Success

Success: What to do (and not do) to be successful in your job

LIBRARY OF CONGRESS CATALOGUING-IN-PUBLICATION DATA

Stuart-Kotze, R.
Success: What to do (and not do) to be successful in your job

ISBN: 978-1-07573-614-8

Success- Psychological aspects
Success in organizations
Interpersonal relations

Cover design by *et al* design consultants, Oxford, UK

Print font: Sitka Text

Success

What to do
(and not do)
to be successful
in your job

Robin Stuart-Kotzé

Reviews of the book

You won't find a better guide to job success than this book. It's full of excellent tips that apply to anyone in any job situation, whether starting off, or moving up the career ladder.
- Peter Nixon, FCPA-CA, Bestselling author of *The Business Developer's Playbook*

This book is extremely practical and I have got a lot of value from it. One of the great things it has done is make me understand stress and how to manage it effectively. I will recommend all my team to read it.
- Valentina Mata, Marketing, Latin America, Netflix

A superbly documented guide covering many essential things for people to understand to achieve job and career success. I will definitely give a copy to my team leaders in setting up a value-added working environment.
- M. B. Wansbrough, Founder, Licensed to Learn Inc.

Based on research fact, this book shows what you need to do master the challenges of any job and be successful.
- Dr Rick Roskin

Companies should give a copy of this book to every one of their new recruits. It gets people on the right track immediately.
- Doug Williams, Training and development consultant

As a relatively young General Manager of an auto dealership, I found this book extremely beneficial for sharpening my skills and developing the performance of my staff. It provides superb insight on how to improve personal performance in so many aspects of business.
- Liam Patey, General Manager, Lansdsperg Auto Group

TO

Dr Peter Honey

Eminent occupational psychologist and prolific author whose work and books have helped thousands of people improve their success and lives. With heartfelt thanks for all the support and advice you've given me on this and other books, and for the warmth of your friendship.

Chris Dunn

A valued colleague and friend, and a behaviour expert who, like Peter Honey, has helped many hundreds of people to have successful and fulfilling careers, and whose insights as we've worked together have shed light on seemingly intractable problems.

Barry Wansbrough and Michaele Robertson

Two brilliant educators whose work with thousands of students each year, in more than 100 secondary schools, prepares them to meet the challenge of becoming the flexible, resilient, self-directed and curious people they need to be, and helps them achieve the best future for themselves.

Table of Contents

INTRODUCTION

You are never a loser until you quit trying
Mike Ditka

What are the secrets of job success? When you start a job you need to learn which actions will make you successful and which will cause you to fail. You need to know how to spot and avoid the many traps of organizational life. You can start from zero and learn the hard way through experience, or you can read this book and learn the key secrets to success, avoid many of the pitfalls, and get on the fast track.

This book will teach you some critically important skills such as:

- how to influence people,
- how to handle pressure and stress,
- how to work well with other people,
- how to select jobs that suit you best,
- how to present yourself effectively,
- what motivates you,
- what to avoid doing

It will tell you things you can apply immediately to your present job and to the various jobs you move into over the length of your career.

There are people who will tell you that you can't get smarter or better, and that in the end, job success is about luck. Don't believe them. They're wrong.

You *can* get smarter and you *can* get better at things. It's not about luck. It's about focus, dedication, and persistence. The famous movie producer Sam Goldwyn said, "The harder I work, the luckier I get", but working hard isn't enough, you need to know what to work hard at – what to do and what not to do.

Malcolm Gladwell said that to become an expert at something takes 10,000 hours of practice.[1] But it's *what* you practice and *how* you practice that matters. You can go to a golf driving range and hit balls for 10,000 hours and never become expert. You will be successful if you practice the right things. No book can tell you everything you need to do because all jobs are different, but there are some essentials and this books shows you what they are.

Fact or fake news?

Unfortunately, we live in an age of fake news and fake facts and it can be difficult to find out whether what is being said or printed is true or not. ***Everything in this book is scientifically-proven fact.***

You will have noticed a little number at the end of a sentence in the previous paragraph. You'll see them all through the book. They are references to the scientific research that proves what has been said. You don't need to read the research articles, but if you want to check whether something is fact, the references prove it.

If you prefer some proof from live people rather than research articles, at the end of each chapter, in a section called *What Successful People Do*, there is a short summary of an interview with an individual who talks about what has made them successful and what advice they have for people starting out in their careers.

THE OUTLINE OF THE BOOK

CHAPTER 1: What are you doing now?

The first step in the journey to job success is to clear your mind of what you think you "know" about job success, but what is, unfortunately, not true. The chapter starts by dealing with four major fallacies that hold many people back from realizing that they can change and be successful. It looks at the dangers of habit and failing to notice changes going on around you, and raises the question of knowing which of your actions have a positive effect and the importance of setting priorities and maintaining focus on them.

CHAPTER 2: What should you be doing differently?

The most important factor determining whether an action is effective or not is the situation in which the action is taken. "the situation" is a broad term that encompasses a wide variety of things like your boss, the people you work with, your customers (including internal customers in your organization), your skill, time demands, and so on. Jobs are continually changing and it's critically important to adapt your behaviour to handle these changes. The chapter gives you a list of important things to do to be successful, and a list of things not to do.

CHAPTER 3: How can you influence things?

Job success is not about position or authority, it's about influencing the perceptions and actions of others. Everything you do has influence. The chapter is about managing people's impressions and judgements of you, and it describes and explains the most important influencing behaviours you can use.

CHAPTER 4: The unconscious influencers

The chapter looks at how, unconsciously, you influence people's impressions of you. it points out the power of non-verbal communication. Non-verbal cues have more than four times the effect of spoken words. Although while you do (mostly subconsciously) things that influence others' actions and emotions, there are also outside influences that effect how *you* act. The chapter examines the fact that while we think the brain runs the body, it also works the other way, and your actions affect what happens in your brain.

CHAPTER 5: Handling pressure and stress

In the fast-moving world of the 21st century very few jobs are free from pressure and stress, and how you react to it can make a big difference between job success or failure. This is immensely important. The chapter looks at how to turn stress into a positive force, and how to manage it effectively.

CHAPTER 6: The causes of stress and your reactions to it

There are two sides to stress, a harmful one and a positive one. People who see it as negative tend to react to pressure and stress in three basic ways – with defensive-aggressive actions, by avoiding conflict, and/or by avoiding responsibility – all of which have negative consequences.

But viewing stress as a positive force does the opposite, and can make you smarter, stronger and more competent. This chapter gives you some helpful tips on how to handle stress.

CHAPTER 7: What motivates you?

Unless you find your job, or at least some aspects of it, motivating, it can be difficult to become successful. Understanding what types of things motivate you is a major key to job success and overall satisfaction. The chapter describes and discusses the most important motivating factors and helps you identify what motivates you and what to look for in jobs that will suit you best.

CHAPTER 8: Working in teams

A lot of work is done in informal or formal teams, and how you work in team settings is important for job success. Teamwork is not always the most effective way to get results and there are a number of reasons why this is the case. The chapter looks at what makes teams operate effectively and how you need to act to be an effective team member.

THANKS

Writing a book is a journey down a long and demanding road and it's easy to stray off course. The book which you are reading is very different from what it started out to be. Charles Dickens may have only written things once, but as every other author knows, getting it right involves not just revisiting and revising what you've written again and again, it also requires comment and feedback from others.

As an author you may think that what you've written is clear and easily understandable, but behind what you say or write is always a huge set of assumptions about what others know and think. Something may sound simple and straightforward to you because of your experience, but it may be gibberish to someone who hasn't shared that experience. Without the feedback, support, and comments from a number of people who gave freely of their time to read early drafts, this book would never have seen the light of day.

Sincere thanks to my old friend from undergraduate university days, Barry Wansbrough, an experienced and outstanding educator and author of *Skillpod, 7 Skills Critical for Working (and Living) in the Digital Age.* Dr. Rick Roskin, my friend from MBA school, an academic colleague and co-author with me of *Managerial Achievement.*

Peter Nixon, long-time friend and colleague, and author of the outstanding books, *The Business Developer's Playbook, Negotiation,* and *The Dialog Gap*; Alejandro Serralde, friend and colleague, and co-author with me of *Los Siete Secretos de los Lideres Altamente Effectivos.*

Peter Honey, eminent occupational psychologist, prolific builder of garden sheds from discarded timber, and author of so many books it would fill the page to list them;

Doug Williams, vastly experienced international trainer and development expert whose work with successful people in a wide variety of occupations and situations helped me maintain focus; Liam Patey, an outstanding young leader who is proof that we're in good hands with the millennial generation; Valentina Mata, another hugely talented millennial who makes it all look deceptively easy; and Lorna, my marvellous wife who never ceases to amaze me with her remarkable insights, whose support and patience is unflagging, and whose feedback is always invaluable.

And a very special thanks to the busy executives who so kindly gave their valuable time to share their experiences with readers of the book: Rafael Mendoza, Nathalie Balda, Colin Patey, Wanda Sevilla Krieb, Rodrigo Azpurua, Andreina Poveda, Jose and Charly Chahin, Bruno Mercenari, and David Hunt. Your contributions are invaluable and I am forever in your debt. Many, many thanks.

Chapter 1

What are you doing now?

The only place success comes before work is in the dictionary.
Vince Lombardi

You're starting on an exciting journey to achieve job success. Are you feeling confident?

Here's a tip to get you off and running – and like everything in this book it is backed by scientific proof.

> ➤ Get a soft rubber ball and gently squeeze it in your right hand for a few minutes. You must use your right hand, no matter whether you're right-handed or left-handed. This action will make you feel more positive by increasing the activity of the left side of your brain, and that's the side of the brain that gets you motivated and eager to achieve things. [2]

Done that? Good. Then let's get started.

What you "know" that isn't true

The first step is to clear your mind of what you think you "know" about job success, but what is, unfortunately, not true. This is going to take some effort on your part because it's a distressing fact that what you think you "know", even though it is proven to be false, still exerts influence on your judgments.

It is difficult – but not impossible - to hit the reset button to erase the false information and substitute the correct facts.[3]

To begin with, do you believe your success or failure is a result of your own efforts, or do you believe that it's a result of things over which you have no control?

The fact is that success is a direct result of your efforts. Understanding that is very important. People who believe their efforts and actions are what makes the difference are higher achievers, more successful, and more satisfied.[4] People who believe it's just about luck and things outside of their control are the opposite.

Four basic fallacies that need to be dismissed

There are four major fallacies that hold many people back from job success.

Fallacy 1: Your brain is hard-wired and unchangeable.

Fact: It's not.[5]
Your brain can be, and is, changed by experiences – both physical and emotional.[6] [7] You *can* become smarter. You *can* develop new skills and you *can* get better at doing things. Here are four simple steps you can take right away that will make you smarter:

> ➢ If you have a problem that you need to solve, don't sit down. Get up and walk around, or go for a walk outside. This will make you more creative and more likely to come up with an answer.[8]

➢ If you want to remember the words of something that's a bit complex like a presentation or speech you're going to make, practice it with movements and gestures and you will remember it much better.[9]

➢ Work to become fitter. The more physically fit you are, the smarter and more successful you become. Research with more than a million young people showed that the fitter they were, the higher their IQ and the higher their probability of job success.[10]

➢ If you need to think creatively, squeeze a soft rubber ball for a few minutes, this time in your *left* hand. That will generate activity in your right brain and that stimulates creativity. [11]

Fallacy 2: *You constantly lose brain cells and get no replacements as you age.*

Fact: Yes, you lose some brain cells but you also constantly generate new ones.
You do lose brain cells as you get older, but you also develop new ones to replace them quite easily. The fact is that older people can think just as divergently as younger people.[12] You develop new brain cells through a process called neurogenesis, and that process is activated by physical exercise. [13]

➢ If you need to focus attention on something, engage in a short (20 minutes or so) of vigorous exercise like a fast walk.[14]

➢ If you want to be able to think more creatively and flexibly about a problem, once again, aerobic exercise helps.[15]

➤ You can become smarter and you can improve your memory, but the interesting thing is that it's not engaging in mentally challenging tasks and so-called "exercising of the brain" things like doing crosswords and puzzles that generates the most new cells, it's doing vigorous physical exercise like going for a run or a good walk.[16] [17]

➤ And you're going to love this: repeated sexual experiences also create new brain cells.

➤ But the improvement disappears after prolonged abstinence, so frequency is important.[18]

Fallacy 3: *You are a prisoner of your genetics.*

Fact: You aren't.
You have about 24,000 genes, and yes, they are yours for life, and yes, their basic structure can't be changed, but *the way they work can be changed, and is changed, by experiences*.[19]

➤ Genes create proteins and these proteins control functions of the brain and body that in turn affect behaviour. Things you experience turn the gene creation of proteins on or off so that you feel and act differently.[20]

➤ The environment you work in affects how you feel and act. It might create stress, challenge, depression, enjoyment, or any number of other effects, and each of these things create gene proteins that change your brain, and hence, your actions.[21]

> When you go through a stressful experience it causes your genes to create a protein that affects your immune system and makes you more susceptible to illness.[22]

Fallacy 4: *Personality predicts performance.*

Fact: Personality predicts, at most, 15% of behaviour: it's what you *do* that determines performance.[23] [24]
Don't confuse behaviour with personality. What you *do* (behaviour) determines your performance, not what you *are* (personality). *It is absolutely critical not to confuse the two things.*

> Your personality is about preference – how you would *prefer* to act, given no constraints. But unfortunately, jobs have lots of constraints. You might prefer to sleep until noon, but if your work starts at 9.00 in the morning you'd better be there at that time if you want to stay on the payroll. You might enjoy dominating people because you allegedly have a "dominant personality", but you better not indulge that preference with your boss. What you might *like* (prefer) to do is not necessarily what you *need* to do.

> Personality is essentially fixed at an early age.[25] Given that we live in an age of continuous and rapid change, if you believe that your personality preferences, which are fixed, are what drives your performance and results, unless the job you're in also remains completely fixed (and that is *highly* unlikely), you're in trouble. But you're not a captive to your personality. You don't *have to* indulge your preferences.

> You have control over what you do. Remember: job success is a result of what you **do**.

> A personality test may give you some insight about yourself, but you need to take the results with a grain of salt because personality tests are notoriously inaccurate. Research shows that 75% of people get a different result when they do a personality test again.[26]

> Add to that the fact that people are amazingly good at finding complimentary things about themselves, and they project these characteristics onto their test results. Bertram Forer gave a group of individuals a personality test and then handed them back their "results". In fact the "results" were randomised astrological forecasts from a book he had bought at a nearby newsstand. When he asked the individuals how accurate they found their profiles on a scale of 0 (poor) to 5 (perfect), 40% gave a perfect 5 and the average score for the group was 4.2. [27]

> When given the results of a personality test people will tend to project themselves on to the positive things it shows. For instance, if you tell people that extroverts are more likely to be successful they will focus on their actions that are extroverted, and if you tell them introverts are more successful they will look for those cues in themselves.[28]

What do you do to achieve results in your job?

In spite of the stupid things people say about "giving 110%", you only have 100% of effort, energy, and attention available to give to anything. You can't expand on 100%. That's it.

So if you use some percentage of your energy and effort to do something, you have to take if from doing something else. One of the most important lessons in life is that you can't do everything. The expression "Jack of all trades and master of none" says it all.

Achieving job success requires that you focus on the actions that are critical and put to one side other less important things that are competing for your attention.[29] In perhaps the most comprehensive study ever done of the determinants of performance, Morten Hansen found that *the principal factor that explains high-level performance is selecting a tiny set of priorities and making huge efforts to achieve them.*[30]

Harvard professor Michael Porter said that strategy was about deciding what *not* to do. Job success is very much like that. We all know the catchphrase for real estate, "Location, location, location". For job success it's "Focus, focus, focus".

Success is also very strongly correlated with conscientiousness.[31] Being conscientious is about wanting to do things properly, to do them well and to do them thoroughly.
You can't be successful if you don't act like that. But being conscientious also has two other *hugely* beneficial consequences: first, conscientious people live longer,[32] and secondly they recover faster and better from major surgery and illness.[33]

Focus on doing the most important things, do them properly and well, and you'll be more successful, you'll be healthier, and you'll live longer.

What's your starting point?

An essential thing you need to know before you begin any journey is where you are to begin with. If you have a GPS system in your car, or a travel app, it can't tell you how to get somewhere unless it knows where you're starting from. So the first thing you need to know as you embark on the journey to achieve job success is what you're doing now. Can you answer this basic question?

What *specific* things are you doing in your job right now to drive your performance and results?

Extensive research shows that while you do lots of different things in your job each day, most of them have little or no impact on your results, and 80% of the results you achieve are due to a small handful of your actions. It is therefore very important that you focus on what those actions are.

Despite what you may have read and heard (and there are thousands of articles, manuals and programs that claim to have "the answer") *there is no magic set of actions that leads unfailingly to success.* It depends on the job you're in, the people you work with, the various things that are happening around you, and so on. You do lots of different things every day in your job or outside work. Some of them have good results and some of them don't.

So, to ask the question in a slightly different way. Can you identify the specific actions you've taken that worked well for you, and the actions that turned out poorly?

Take a few minutes now to think about that, and make lists of what has worked well for you and what has not.

The time spent doing this will have a good payoff. This is critical information on which you will build your platform of success.

The dangers of habit

Your brain works at two basic levels, your conscious brain and your unconscious brain. The conscious brain is slow and lazy relative to the unconscious brain. The conscious brain processes about 120 bits of information per second; the unconscious brain processes 11 *million* bits per second.[34]
It processes entire images in just 13 milliseconds.[35] Because the conscious brain is slow and because it absorbs a lot of energy, it tries to economize and becomes lazy.
It tends to overlook small changes that begin to signal the need to act differently, and that turns actions that once worked well for you into habits that may no longer be applicable.

Deep in your brain, toward the centre of your skull, is a golf ball sized part of the brain called the basal ganglia. Among other things it's a part of the brain that develops habits.[36] More than 40% of the things you do each day are habit.[37] Things become habit through experience, and they become reinforced each time you do them. You feel comfortable with them, so you tend to favour them unless you're somehow shocked out of them. When you fall into a comfortable routine, your brain stops fully focusing on scanning the environment and making appropriate decisions. Unconsciously, because all people, you included, have a strong need for consistency, you continue to do some things in spite of the fact that they have negative consequences.[38]

Think about your trip to work each day. The first time you did it your brain was working at full power, absorbing and processing all the new information – turn here, go up there, enter here, move to the left here, stop there, etc. The second time you took the route you found it's easier, and after a while it became automatic.

If you travel somewhere new that's a distance away, do you find that getting there seems to take longer than getting back home? This is the basal ganglia at work.

You have to work harder to think about the way to get to your destination initially, but when you come back you've already done the hard thinking and the journey is easier.

Each successive time you make the journey your brain has to work less because it's registered the pattern of the trip. That's why you often get somewhere and find you can't really remember the journey, or why sometimes when you're not going to your customary destination and your mind is elsewhere, you find you've made a usual turning and not the one you needed to make. You get the sense you were travelling on "automatic pilot", and you were.

Your brain is constantly looking at ways to save energy and effort. It weighs about three pounds (1.4 kilos), which is around 2% of average body weight. But it consumes 20% of all the energy your body uses. When you pay attention to something you have to make the effort to shift your attention from something else, and that takes energy.[39]

Very few people have the ability to even concentrate on more than one thing at a time, let alone a whole range of things.

If you had to focus constant attention on everything that's happening around you, you'd collapse from the overload. Some processes have to be "packaged" and stored so they can be accessed without effort. The process is called chunking.[40] The upside of chunking is that the brain doesn't have to exercise itself to make a number of difficult decisions – they've already been made. The downside is that it can blind you to the need to be aware of changes to the situation that require different decisions and actions.

However, there is an even more dangerous downside to the chunking of a set of actions or reactions: a habit that you worked at changing never completely disappears.[41] It remains somewhere in your memory. Your brain retains a memory of the context of the habit. For example, you used to regularly stop on the way to work to get a coffee and a pastry or muffin or something to go along with the coffee, and you're now trying to break the habit. Every time you stop to get a coffee you have to make the conscious decision not to get a snack. To make sure you follow your intention to avoid the snack, you need to create what psychologists call an "implementation intention.[42] If you actually say to yourself each time you set out for work, "When I stop for a coffee I will not buy a cake or pastry, or snack of any kind", you will create a new unconscious context and control the habit.

What Successful People Do

Rafael Mendoza
CEO, Astra Zeneca
(Colombia, Peru, Ecuador, and Venezuela)

"The key thing everyone needs to remember", Rafael says, "is that you can change and make of yourself what you want". He talks about fully realizing that when he made a major presentation to an important group of people and it fell flat. He felt he'd failed and was discouraged and down. But he happened to hear a singer he liked do a song that was completely different from his usual style. "That moment was a revelation to me", he says. "It showed me that you don't have to keep doing the same thing and it made me realize that I could reinvent myself".

One of the lessons he learned from that was that even from the greatest frustrations you can learn something, and if you take that learning to heart you can change. The corporate world, he says, requires people who can change. It requires flexibility. Every business is changing rapidly and it's essential that people are able to change with it.

Rafael has built highly effective work teams in Latin America, Asia, the United States, and Europe.

When he hires someone, he avoids people who are trapped by the type of thinking that the fallacies listed in this chapter describe: that your brain is unchangeable and you can't become smarter, that you are a prisoner of your genetics, and that your personality determines your actions.

"These fallacies", he says, "prevent the rapid learning and ability to cope with change that are essential for success".

He offers this tip for dealing with situations that don't go well. If, for instance, he has a difficult meeting he takes a break and goes for a walk. This, he says, helps him relax and relieve tension. Every day has some ups and some downs, and Rafael says it helps to take a longer term view. Sometimes you have a bad experience, but, he says, "it doesn't define your existence. You also have good experiences. The most important thing to remember is that you can learn from both the bad experiences and the good ones. If you can do that you will be successful".

His advice to people is to ask yourself the question, "What has worked well for me, and what has not?" You learn from experience, so make every experience a learning opportunity.

Key points from this chapter

There are four major fallacies that hold many people back from job success.

Fallacy 1: Your brain is hard-wired and unchangeable.

Fact: Your brain can be, and is, changed by physical experiences and emotional experiences. You *can* become smarter. You *can* develop new skills and you *can* get better at doing things.

> ➤ If you have a problem that you need to solve, don't sit down. Get up and walk around, or go for a walk outside. This will make you more creative and more likely to come up with an answer.

> ➤ If you want to remember the words of something that's a bit complex like a presentation or speech you're going to make, practice it with movements and gestures and you will remember it much better.

> ➤ Work to become fitter. The more physically fit you are, the smarter and more successful you become.

> ➤ If you need to think creatively, squeeze a soft rubber ball for a few minutes, this time in your *left* hand. That will generate activity in your right brain and that stimulates creativity.

Fallacy 2: : You constantly lose brain cells and get no replacements as you age.

Fact: You lose brain cells as you get older, but you also develop new ones to replace them quite easily through physical exercise.

- ➢ Going for a fast walk helps you
  - Focus attention
  - Think creatively and flexibly
  - Improve you memory

Fallacy 3: You are a prisoner of your genetics.

Fact: Your basic gene *structure* can't be changed, but *the way the genes work can be changed, and is changed, by experiences.*

- ➢ Things you experience turn the gene creation of proteins on or off so that you feel and act differently.

- ➢ When you go through a stressful experience it causes your genes to create a protein that affects your immune system and makes you more susceptible to illness.

Fallacy 4: Personality predicts performance.

Fact: The thing that drives performance is *behaviour* – how you act. Personality only predicts 10-15% of your performance in any circumstance.

- ➢ 80% of the results you do achieve are due to a small handful of your actions.

- ➢ There is no magic set of actions that leads unfailingly to success.

- ➢ Achieving job success requires that you focus on the critical actions and put to one side other less important things that are competing for your attention.

- The principal factor that explains high-level performance is selecting a tiny set of priorities and making huge efforts to achieve them

- Success is also very strongly correlated with conscientiousness

- Focus on doing the most important things, do them properly and well, and you'll be more successful, you'll be healthier, and you'll live longer.

The dangers of habit

- More than 40% of the things you do each day are habit.

- Unconsciously, because all people, you included, have a strong need for consistency, you continue to do some things in spite of the fact that they have negative consequences.

Before you leave this chapter, take a few minutes to think about, and write down your answers to these two questions:

1. What *specific* things are you're doing in your job right now to drive your performance and results?

2. What has worked well for you and what has not?

The time spent doing this will have a good payoff. This is critical information on which you will build your platform of success.

Chapter 2

What should you be doing differently?

There is nothing so useless as doing efficiently
that which should not be done at all
Peter Drucker

Where have we got to so far?

> ➤ So far on the journey to achieving job success we began by clearing away some of the things that were blocking the road – some basic fallacies that hinder achieving job success.

> ➤ And we gave you some hints and tips about things you can do to become smarter, become more creative, feel more confident, and be happier and more positive.

> ➤ We pointed out that you need to focus on the specific actions that have the most impact and that drive 80% of your performance and results.

> ➤ We talked about the danger of falling into easy routine and habit.

The next step – What do you need to do differently?

Good results come from doing the right things and poor results come from doing the wrong things. But the question is, "What are the right things"?

That's not a simple question to answer because every situation has a different set of "right things". Your job situation is specific to you, so your "right things" are also unique to you.

> The effectiveness of any action depends on the situation. [43] Nobody behaves the same way in all contexts; the external situation matters. [44]

> That is such an important and absolutely critical thing to understand that we will repeat it: The effectiveness of any action depends on the situation.

> As a result, the effectiveness of your behaviour depends on the accuracy of your reading of the situation. *Always think about the situation and how best to adapt your behaviour to maximise the chances of success.*

Here are some examples of the power of situational factors in determining how people act:

> Larger numbers have a different effect on behaviour than smaller numbers. When people were asked how much they'd spend on dinner in two restaurants, "Studio 17" or "Studio 97", they said they'd pay more in "Studio 97". [45]

> When people are making medical appointments, if they are asked to write down the date and time of the appointment, they are 20% less likely to miss the appointment. [46]

➤ Wearing fake luxury products makes the wearer more likely to behave dishonestly and see other people as being unethical.[47]

➤ When people enter a library or a place of worship they are generally quieter.[48]

➤ You assign more significance to, and pay more attention to, things you see yourself moving towards.[49] So when you're talking to a person, lower your voice when you want them to pay attention to an important point; they will need to lean in towards you and that will focus their interest.

➤ The more greenery people can see from their homes or places of work the less aggressive they become. And their working memory improves.[50]

If those examples of how the situation affects people's behaviour haven't convinced you, this one most definitely will. Students at the Princeton Theological Seminary were asked to read a short text about acts of care and charity (e.g. the parable of the Good Samaritan who stopped to help an injured man after others had ignored him and passed by) and to prepare a five-minute talk about what they had read.[51] The "talk" was to be presented and recorded in another, unfamiliar, building, so that when the students had done their preparation they were told to follow directions about how to get to the location for their speech.

In situation one, when they had finished reading and preparing their speech, the students were told they were already late for their presentations and needed to hurry to the other building.

In situation two, the students were told there was no rush and they had time to spare.

Remember that these are theological students and they have been reading about and preparing to give a speech about acts of care and charity, so you would expect them, whether they are in a hurry or not, to provide care and help if they happened on a situation where that was clearly required.

On the route the students needed to take to make their presentations, the experimenters placed a person slumped in a doorway and very clearly in need of help and perhaps medical attention. And here's the power of the situation to affect behaviour: the students who were told they needed to hurry were *six times more likely* to keep on walking past the "injured" person than the ones who had lots of time.

The need to adapt your behaviour to the changing situation

Do you notice all the changes in your job situation? You notice the big ones like getting a new boss, but do you notice the little ones? There are all sorts of things going on every day, but you're busy and you don't see them all. As you go to work each day, do you notice the changes along the way – maybe a new sign, different cars, a shop that's gone, a new tree, etc. No, you don't, because you're thinking about other things. Your attention is diverted from small and subtle changes. It's what psychologists call *change blindness*.

An amusing little experiment on a city street demonstrates it well. A researcher posing as a tourist and holding a street map approaches a random pedestrian, hands them the map and asks them for directions. While the person is looking at the map, another individual carrying a wooden door walks between the researcher and the person looking at the map. As that happens, the researcher walks away behind the door and is replaced by someone who looks and sounds completely different. Half the people in the experiment don't notice any change in the person they have been talking to.[52]

At a *conscious* level, you may not notice little changes, but at an *unconscious* level you do. The pre-frontal cortex (PFC) is the most evolved section of the brain, and it enables you to alter your actions and strategies as the situation you face changes – if you let it.

However, while unconsciously you see everything, as Daniel Kahneman points out in his excellent book *Thinking, Fast and Slow*, your conscious brain prefers to take a lazier approach, and it overlooks things that may require more effort or thought.[53] Being alert to tiny changes around you takes effort, so you concentrate on what is more obvious and immediate, and you miss what's occurring.

Change is often gradual and imperceptible. But as the situation changes, if you aren't able to change your behaviour appropriately, your effectiveness declines. As the diagram below illustrates, the more you're able to match your actions to what the situation requires you to do, the greater your probability of job success.

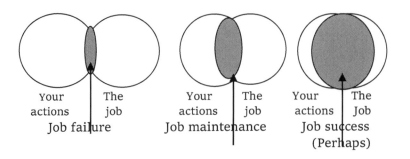

Your job, whether you work for an organization or are self-employed, changes continually. As a result, if you want to stay in the game you have to behave differently – do more of some things or less of some things; stop doing some things, start doing some new things.

Take a break from reading now and list the things that have changed in your job over the past twelve months. Think of the different things you're now required to do and the things you no longer do. Do you have different colleagues, a different boss, different work hours, different responsibilities, different customers or clients, a different work place, different machinery or technology, etc.? Ask a colleague what changes they've noticed. The list of changes will surprise you.

If you think that you're on top of your job right now and you couldn't do it any better, you've probably just fallen behind.

Why people change

People change for one of two reasons: either they see the benefit and want to change (they see the light) or they're forced to change (they feel the heat). Far and away the best strategy is the former – changing because you see the benefit and you want to move forward. The problem with changing only when the heat becomes uncomfortable is that it's often a matter of "too little too late".

In his excellent book *Bringing out the Best in People*,[54] Aubrey Daniels makes this important point: *behaviour is a function of its consequences*. In other words, if doing something will have a positive result you are likely to do it, and if it continues to have positive consequences you are likely to continue doing it.

The supermodel Kate Moss got a lot of criticism when she said, "Nothing tastes as good as skinny feels". But she was simply stating that the behaviour of not tucking into doughnuts, chocolates, cakes, etc. has a good consequence for her. She remains slim, and remaining slim is central to her success as a model.

While you're likely to continue to do things that have a positive result for you, it's important not to carry on blindly doing something without looking at what may have changed in the situation. You see examples in sports all the time. Individuals and teams carry on with what has proved to be a winning technique but fail to recognize that their opponents have adapted their response, and their performance falls. The situation has changed but the behaviour hasn't.

One of the problems in deciding whether to continue doing something or to change is what's known as the *self-serving bias*. It's when you assume that your successes are due to your intelligence and expertise and your failures are due to someone else, or just bad luck.

> ➤ *You are what you learn.* Every failure is an opportunity to learn. Blaming it on someone or something else will not help you succeed in your work or your life. Be careful, because the more your bad performance or failure is bruising to your ego, the more likely you are to fall into the self-serving bias trap.[55]

> ➤ Look at the results of what you do and get feedback about it. If you don't do that how can you judge whether you're doing the right things or the wrong things, and how can you improve?

> And beware of the danger of habit. It's easy to fall into an unthinking routine and when you do that your performance starts to drop.[56]

What do you need to do differently?

How you behave when you start a new job makes a big difference.

> Show interest and commitment by asking questions. People who do these things get more help and support from their boss and important others.[57]

Here are some research-proven suggestions for working better and smarter.

> Take exercise. You don't have to go to the gym every day (but if you are doing that, keep it up), just take a brisk walk for 30 minutes, five days a week.
>   - Exercise prevents aging and brain decline and strengthens your immune system.[58]
>   - It increases your happiness.[59]
>   - It maintains your mental health.[60]
>   - It increases your memory.[61]

> If you're very nervous about doing something, take 10 minutes and write down what's worrying you. That "downloads" your worries and allows you to proceed with the action with much less fear and anxiety.[62]

> When you're faced with a big task and are under time pressure to complete it, a highly useful approach is to use some sort of timer and do the following:

- Set the timer for 25 minutes and focus completely on the task for that length of time.
- When the timer signals the end of the 25 minutes take a 5-minute break.
- Resent the time for another 25 minutes and once again when the timer sounds, take another 5-minute break.
- Do that four times and then take a 30-minute break.
- Start the cycle again and do it one more time, giving you about 4 hours of focused work. Then do something else for the rest of the day and start again tomorrow with another two 4-stage cycles.
- The reason we suggest you stop at the four-hour mark is that research shows that after that your productivity drops off rapidly.

➢ If you're interviewing for a job and are given the choice of doing so either via a video connection or face-to- face, choose the latter. Physical distance relates to psychological distance; the closer you are the more likely you will be able to relate to someone, and vice-versa.

➢ If you're struggling with a difficult problem, take a break. Research shows that increases the probability of finding the solution.[63]

➢ Chances are you live in an urban environment. It's estimated that in little more than a decade about two-thirds of the world's population will live in cities. But cities are filled with things happening to divert your attention. If you want to improve your concentration and there's a park or some green space near you, take a walk there and it will focus your attention more.[64]

➢ But parks don't exist in crowded office buildings or towers or busy city centre streets, so put some pictures of tranquil scenes on your phone and take a ten-minute break and look at them.[65]

➢ Do the most important, or the most difficult, or the most unpleasant thing that needs to be done, first thing in the morning. The reason is that you only have a finite amount of willpower. It's a limited resource and you deplete it as you use it.[66] As the day goes on and you've chipped away at your willpower, it becomes more and more difficult to engage tough problems or tasks, and you keep putting them off.

➢ If you schedule when you'll do something, and you write it down, you're more likely to do it and to complete it.[67]

➢ If you can arrange it, being outside in natural, non-urban settings reduces the tendency to procrastinate, while urban environments do the opposite.[68]

➢ Think about why you put off doing something. Is it to avoid, or at least delay, putting your skill, ability, competence, or reputation for success at risk? [69]

➢ When you're engaging something complex or difficult it's easy to be diverted by something more superficial, which is what makes the constant flow of items on social media so addictive.[70] Resist the temptation to move to these things, and maintain focus on the important task you're engaged in.

➢ Add routines to your life that remove the issue of willpower, and follow these routines.

➢ If you set aside certain times for certain tasks each day you are less likely to be diverted. [71]

➢ Also, as we've shown, your environment has an effect. Make where you work, and for how long, a routine. Use specific locations for some things and other locations for other tasks or activities. Do work in a work area without distraction if you can, not somewhere with all kinds of things going on around you. This helps you focus.

Set some rules about how you'll work

➢ For instance, put your phone on mute, place it in a drawer out of sight, and only look at it at set times during the day.

➢ Take a quick break every hour.[72] Get up from your work and, if you can, walk around your work area for a minute or two and then get back to your task.
➢ If you can get away from your work environment and take a walk, preferably in a quiet place, for as little as ten minutes, your focus of attention will increase.[73]

➢ When you make a mistake, own up to it. You will be trusted much more. When doctors in a hospital were open to patients about medical errors, malpractice suits for the hospital dropped by almost two-thirds.[74]

Re-design your work

That may sound like something that maybe your boss could do, or your boss's boss, but not something over which you have any influence. But that's not necessarily true. There are various ways that you can change your work situation.

➢ Take a few minutes now and make a list of what you're required to do in your job. There will be some things on the list that only you can do and must do. But there are also probably some things that could be done by someone else with whom you work. You can change your job by trading with that person – they do X for you and you do Y for them.

➢ Organize the things on your list into

1) what has to be done, no matter what,
2) what needs to be done but is not urgent, and
3) what would be good to do but isn't particularly important.

That will give you a structure for your work. Make sure you do the things in the first list first before you move to the second list. And make sure you do the things on the second list before you move to the third list.

If you have something big to do, break it into doable chunks

➢ When you do this, several things happen. First, you get a sense of achievement and reward when a segment of the task is completed.

➢ Second, when you finish a piece of work you are able to step back and look at it to see if you're happy with it or if you need to make some change or adjustment. That stops you from getting too far down the road before you discover that something was done incorrectly earlier. You end up with a better end product.

➢ In addition, you develop a greater overall level of expertise because being actively involved in the doing-inspecting-adjusting sequence results in the learning being more strongly encoded in your memory.[75]

Make a note of things when they occur to you

➢ Each time you think of something that you need to do, or that answers a problem, or is an idea that's worth exploring further, put it on a memo. Only one item per memo. That way you can easily sort them into levels of importance. And writing things down when they occur to you – or recording them on your phone and then writing them down later - gets them out of your mind and stops them interfering with what you're trying to focus on.[76] It saves mental energy that you would waste worrying that you might forget.

> The brain can only attend to a very small number of things at a time.[77] So to be effective, make lists of things you need to do or remember.

> Sort them into priorities and when you've dealt with whatever is on a memo screen, you can dispose of it. (If you prefer, you can do the same thing with index cards.)

> One of the bonuses of immediately writing things down as they occur to you is that some of your best ideas come to you seemingly "out of the blue" when you're doing something unrelated.[78] Don't lose them.

Take a step back and think about your longer-term goals

If you don't have an idea of where you want to go, you just end up rambling around randomly.

> Research shows that two things, perseverance and a focus on longer-term goals, have a significant effect on the achievement of job success.[79]

> A study of MBA graduates of Harvard Business School showed that ten years later those people who had made written goals and plans earned ten times as much as the rest of the class.

Take power naps – if you can

- ➤ We'll talk about the negative effects of sleep deprivation and long hours, but research also shows the other side of things – the highly positive effects to be gained by power napping.[80]

- ➤ It expands memory, creates significant cognitive improvement, and results in increased productivity. And the more intellectual the work or challenge, the greater the payoff from power napping.[81]

- ➤ We'll mention this again in the chapter about dealing with pressure and stress, but it's worthwhile pointing out here as well. If you have just been the subject of, or exposed to, angry, threatening, frightening, upsetting behaviour, having a short nap can transform the negative emotions into more positive ones.[82]

- ➤ And here's a further bonus. Taking a nap also reduces the incidence of heart attack, diabetes, and stroke.[83]

- ➤ We know that not everyone is able to take short naps. It's a learned skill. If it's something you can't do, try meditation which is something than can be learned.

Take your allocated vacation time

> ➤ Research done over a 40-year period shows that people who only take a short vacation have a 37% higher chance of dying early. People who take shorter vacations also tend to work more and sleep less well.[84]

> ➤ More than half of Americans don't use all their allocated vacation days. On average they forfeit two full days that can't be rolled over or paid out. People who take 11 or more vacation days are more likely to get a raise or bonus.[85]

> ➤ But plan your vacation at least a month ahead of time because studies show that otherwise the holiday doesn't improve your energy levels or reduce stress.[86]

> ➤ Taking planned vacations a distance from home and not responding to email or phone contact from work improves your health and overall life satisfaction.[87]

Things you need to stop doing

One of the most important questions you need to ask yourself is "what do I need to do less of, or stop doing?" As we said earlier, a key to success in any job is being able to focus on the most important issues and not wasting your time on things that don't make a difference.

Stop working continued long hours

Research shows that working continued long hours negatively affects your job performance, your health and your relationships. For instance,

- ➤ People who work more than 55 hours a week have a 33% increased risk of stroke compared with those who work a 35- to 40-hour week, and they also have a 13% increased risk of coronary heart disease.[88]

- ➤ Performance per hour worked starts to level out at 50 hours per week and declines after that.[89] Just a 10% increase in overtime results in a 2.4% fall in productivity.[90]

- ➤ Doing "all-nighters" or cutting back sleep time does not make you more productive!
- ➤ Sleep is absolutely critical for high-level performance. The National Sleep Foundation says adults need an average of 6-10 hours, i.e. 8 hours.

- ➤ Working continual long hours has a negative effect on cognitive performance – it makes you dumber.[91]

- ➤ Sleep deprivation causes an increased level of the stress hormone cortisol and increases memory deficits and the aging process.[92]

- ➤ Sleep deprivation increases hunger and appetite while at the same time impairing carbohydrate tolerance, doubling down the effect of those cakes, donuts, and cookies and increasing the risk of obesity and diabetes.[93]

➢ Sleep is one of the most critically important factors affecting productivity, memory, performance, and immune function. Even going to bed late one night and then sleeping in the next morning can have a negative effect on your performance for days afterwards.[94]

➢ A good night's sleep more than doubles the probability that you will come up with a solution to a problem that's been bothering you and that requires insight.[95]

➢ Sleep deprivation is associated with heart disease, stroke and cancer.[96]

➢ Sleeping pills interfere with memory and have a similar effect to sleep deprivation.[97]

➢ At the end of a 12-hour or longer workday, 45% of people are too tired to say anything at all to their spouses or partners.[98]

➢ And here's a little fact that you'll find interesting, and you might want to bear in mind if you're being hounded to work extreme hours. A research study found that bosses couldn't tell the difference between people who worked 80 hours per week and those who pretended to.[99]

Manage and cut back on time spent on emails and social media

➢ If your day begins with having to deal with a large number of "urgent" emails and messages, your clarity of focus and attention will decline.[100]

➢ The problem with emails and social media is that they're addictive. The average professional spends six hours a day on emails.[101]

➢ People check their email an average of 74 times a day.[102] The reason why this occurs is that the brain is attracted by novelty and each time you receive a text or an email or tweet, it's a novelty. In addition, when you reply to it in some form or other you get a feeling of "reward" for having completed a task, and that gives you a shot of dopamine, "the reward/pleasure hormone". Because you get a pleasurable sensation, you crave more.

➢ Along with the dopamine hits, social media also increases the levels of cortisol, the stress hormone, in your system. When active Facebook users were compared with individuals who gave up Facebook for five days, the ones who continued to use it were shown to have significantly higher stress levels.[103]

➢ Twitter is a major emotional arouser and burns a lot of energy as you constantly switch attention from one thing to another.[104]

> Tweeting and re-tweeting raises arousal by 75%, indicated by pulse rate increase, increased perspiration, and enlarged pupils, while simply reading your own Tweets raises arousal by 65%.[105]

> E-mail is also a work stressor; 92% of people show elevated blood pressure and heart rate when using email at work.[106]

> It's recommended that you deal with your emails two or three times a day in batches, rather than attending to them as they come in.[107]

Stop thinking you can multi-task effectively. You can't.

> Attention is a limited capacity resource. If you pay attention to one thing it means you can't pay attention to something else. Multi-tasking decreases productivity, hampers creativity, and causes increased mistakes and errors.[108]

> People may tell you they're good at multi-tasking, but research makes it absolutely clear that they are deluding themselves.[109] They have poorer memory [110], are poorer organizers [111], and are slower at completing tasks effectively.[112]

> Multi-tasking actually makes you dumber. Trying to learn information while multi-tasking causes the information you're trying to learn to go into the wrong part of the brain, and it is more difficult to remember.[113]

➢ Research shows that if you're trying to concentrate on a task and you are aware of an unread email in your inbox, your IQ at that point will drop by ten points.[114]

➢ Multi-tasking tires you significantly. Making a series of decisions about different things, and switching from one task or situation to another causes neural fatigue. It is literally an energy drain, and leads to making poor and impulsive decisions.[115]

➢ Multi-tasking also pumps cortisol into your brain and that increases your likelihood of engaging in impulsive or aggressive behaviours.[116]

➢ Staying focused on one task takes much less energy and reduces the brain's need for glucose.[117]

What Successful People Do

Nathalie Balda
Senior Marketing Manager, Amazon Prime

Nathalie has had an interesting and challenging career. She began her work career focused on digital marketing and social media and, among other things, worked in HBO with *Game of Thrones*.

She set up a blog about food and restaurants in Miami called *Miami Food Porn*. It has over 130,000 followers on Instagram. She ran a number of award winning campaigns at Netflix. She is now a senior marketing manager at Amazon Prime.

She's also hit some bumps along the way and had some failures, but, she says. "The progress of my career is due to the mistakes I've made". She stresses that it's important to get feedback about your performance. Without feedback on how you're doing it's impossible to improve. She credits the culture of Netflix, which encourages constant feedback and dialogue, for helping her become more aware and to continually grow professionally. She says her mantra is, "The road to success is paved with failure", but the key thing about failing is to learn from it and not make the same mistake again.

There are always some things in every job that you don't like doing but are necessary. Her advice to people is to openly identify these things and work out a method of dealing with them effectively.

She says, "It's better to be honest and acknowledge that there are things we simply don't like doing. When I have to do something I dislike, I reward myself a little." She recommends doing the most difficult tasks first to get them out of the way so you can concentrate on the more important things.

Nathalie is an excellent example of someone who understands the need to be constantly aware of the changing situation. She maintains a high level of performance by adapting her actions to allow her to focus on the important elements of each task she takes on. She looks for work on challenging, unique projects that make her move outside her comfort zone.

But she also recognizes the importance of being able to step away from work and do something completely different. She says it's important to switch off from time to time, and vacations are fundamental for goal achievement. She says she always plans her vacations ahead of time to ensure that they give her a complete break from her work.

Key points from this chapter:

➢ Good results come from doing the right things and poor results come from doing the wrong things.

➢ The effectiveness of any action depends on the situation.

➢ Your situation is a combination of various factors that affect how you behave – your goals, your skills, your tasks, the people you work with, your boss, technology, competition, quality requirements, time demands, etc.

➢ There are all sorts of things going on every day, but you're busy, and you don't see them all. At a *conscious* level, you may not notice little changes, but at an *unconscious* level you do.

➢ As the situation changes if you aren't able to change your behaviour appropriately your effectiveness declines.

➢ The greater the match between your actions and what the situation requires you to do, the greater your probability of job success.

➢ People change for one of two reasons: either they see the benefit and want to (they see the light) or they're forced to (they feel the heat).

➢ Behaviour is a function of its consequences. In other words, if doing something will have a positive result you are likely to do it, and if it continues to have positive consequences you are likely to continue doing it.

What do you need to do differently?

The list of suggestions is too long to repeat here. Put a tab on the section so you can refer to it quickly.

➢ Re-design how you work

➢ Break large pieces of work into doable chunks

➢ Make a note when you think of something or need to do something

➢ Think about your longer-term goals

➢ Take power naps, or if you can't, try meditating

➢ Take all your vacation time

What do you need to stop doing?

➢ Stop working continued long hours.

➢ Manage and cut back on time spent on emails and social media.

➢ Stop thinking you can multi-task effectively. You can't.

Chapter 3

How can you influence things?

*The humblest individual exerts some
influence upon others*
Henry Ward Beecher

You influence things by what you do. It's your actions, conscious and unconscious, that determine whether you're successful or not. People see what you do, and they hear what you say. Everything you do has an influence. You're never too small, or too junior. The late Anita Roddick put it nicely when she said, "If you think you're too small to have an impact, try going to sleep with a mosquito in the room".

How do you exert influence?

First of all, to exert influence you have to want to. That sounds a bit stupid doesn't it? Who doesn't want to influence some things? But you may not believe that you can. This is really important because if you believe that you can have influence over things, that you can become smarter, more competent and more successful if you work at it, you're likely to be successful. Henry Ford said, "Whether you think you can or think you can't, you're right". Research shows that Henry was correct: people who think they can, succeed, and people who think they can't, don't.[118]

Secondly, in order to have influence you need to be noticed.[119] You need to stand out. The more people see you and see what you've done, the more they remember you, and the more positive their attitudes to you become.[120]

Of course that assumes that you do positive things. Being a highly visible jerk is not a recommended strategy for success. Don't be boastful and a show-off. Research shows that boastful people are the least effective and that a middle-ground mix of competence and modesty is viewed most positively by others.[121]

Thirdly, you need to project confidence and a sense of power. We're not talking about dominance, just the sense that you have confidence and control over yourself. Research shows that when you feel powerless you perform poorly, but when you feel you have some control over what's going on, you perform better.[122]

One of the reasons for this is that when you feel confident about something you're more likely to make an effort to make it occur. This is your left brain at work, making you feel more in control and more focused on achievement.[123] So if you want to boost your confidence, remember our tip at the beginning of the book, to squeeze a soft rubber ball in your right hand, because it activates the left brain.

The opposite happens when you feel powerless and lacking in confidence. It's your right brain at work, and it's associated with caution and meekness[124] and you're less willing to risk doing something.[125] (However, squeezing a rubber ball in you left hand doesn't make you meek, so getting an opponent to do that doesn't work.)

There is a warning notice attached to confidence though. You need to avoid overconfidence because it tends to get you to overlook various things, to miss important facts, and to end up making bad decisions.[126] The key is to feel confident but not cocky.

The major influencers

Reciprocation – giving back

Perhaps the most powerful influencing factor is reciprocation. Humans have an underlying, compelling need to reciprocate for any gift or favour they receive. It's deeply embedded in virtually all cultures. We believe that we should reciprocate when someone does something for us. If someone does you a favour you should return the favour; if someone gives you a gift you should try to give them a gift in return, and so on.

If you think this occurs only when the person likes you but not when they don't, you would be wrong. The fact is that simply giving someone even some small thing hugely increases the likelihood of them doing you a favour in return, whether they like you or not.[127]

The act of reciprocation provides them with a good feeling about themselves – they like themselves more. The proof that it's this positive feeling that generates the behaviour is demonstrated by the fact that when a giver refuses to accept a reciprocal gift or favour of any kind, he or she is disliked.[128] The giver has prevented you from feeling good about yourself by being able to give something back.

The key to this method of influence is to do the favour or give the gift *unsolicited* – no strings attached. It's not the same as promising to do something or giving something on condition of the other party's actions – "I will give you X if you do Y". That's more in the nature of doing a deal and the issue of reciprocity doesn't kick in.

Doing things for people without them asking is a major factor in job success. A study of engineers at a big telecoms company found that the most productive engineers were the ones who gave help and assistance more often, and gave more than they received. Not only did they have the highest level of productivity, but they were also the most admired by their peers. [129]

Contrast - a twist on reciprocation

The principle of contrast is that when you see two things that are different, one after the other, you tend to see the second one as more different than it actually is. For instance, if you see something with a high price and then something with a lower price, the second item seems cheaper than it is. If you ask someone to lend you a largish amount of money, say something like a hundred dollars, and they don't want to and are hesitant, if you then ask them to lend you twenty, the probability of them giving you the money is greatly increased.[130] The reason is that the person you have asked views your move from asking for a hundred to asking for twenty as a concession – a "gift" in some sense – and they feel the need to reciprocate.

Robert Cialdini, a leading expert on the psychology of influence, ran a series of experiments with a group of colleagues to explore this phenomenon.[131] They first asked a random sample of 72 individuals if they would agree to an extreme request - chaperone a group of juvenile delinquents for a day trip to the zoo. Needless to say, the vast majority refused. But when these people were first asked if they would agree to spending two hours a week for two years counselling juvenile delinquents, and then asked if they would agree to the smaller request – the zoo trip – three times as many agreed.

Put that into the context of a job, and if you want someone to do something, begin by asking for something bigger, then concede that it's not possible and ask for something smaller. But the key, in terms of job success, is to maintain and grow the relationship. That means you need to know you can, and will, do something in return. When you reciprocate, it strengthens the bond, and everyone wins.

Conformity

You tend to do what other people in your reference group (the people whom you see as sharing similar values, similar tastes, similar backgrounds, etc.) do, and you tend to believe that what they believe is correct. The greater the number of people in your reference group who do something, the more that influences your actions. Psychologists call it *social influence*. The more people who buy something, the more other people want it. Sales of new model iPhones in the first three days of launch in 2010 were 1.7 million. They were 4 million in 2011, 5 million in 2012, 9 million in 2013, and 14 million in 2014.

In 2017 the new phone sold out in ten minutes on the first day. Sales have flattened now, perhaps because of price, but more likely because the market is saturated – everyone has a phone (see "scarcity" below).

Social media has created a new category of people – "influencers". These are people with whom you would like to identify – would like in some way to be like.
They provide reviews about all kinds of things and their views influence their followers to buy or try whatever they promote. We're influenced by all kinds of endorsements and reviews. A common example is movie reviews; positive reviews have a major effect on box office revenue.[132] Restaurant reviews act the same way.

If you're watching a live performance and you start applauding at the end of a scene or song, the rest of the audience will start to applaud. This fact was well known and used in ancient Greek theatre where authors of plays salted hired people through an audience to clap or laugh at various points. The Roman emperor Nero took it to an extreme and created a school of applause so that when he gave concerts he had 5,000 paid people in the audience to applaud him. Canned laughter on TV shows is nothing new.

If you want someone to agree to something or do something, it's helpful if you can show that it's what others have done or are doing. Your argument is strengthened further if the reference group to which you refer are similar to the individual you're trying to influence. That makes it easier for the person you're trying to influence to relate to and identify with them.

Similarity - an element of conformity

We like people who are similar to us – similar background, education, opinions, friends, associations, life-style, language, culture, etc. In a job, it's useful to try to find out about the backgrounds and interests of colleagues and bosses. The strength of a social bond is a powerful source of influence.

People who relate to one another dress similarly and behave in a similar fashion. At work, if the common dress code for women is to wear a dress or skirt, or for men to wear a jacket and collared shirt, despite that perhaps not being your thing it's not a bad idea to conform to some degree. Research shows that your appearance strongly influences other people's perception of your success, authority, trustworthiness, intelligence, and suitability for hire or promotion.[133] One of the reasons is that how you dress gives signals about your social and organizational standing.[134] Clothing and grooming can have a stronger effect on hiring decisions than qualifications.

You also like and trust people more when they look somewhat like you. During a political campaign, individuals were shown photographs of two male "candidates" they hadn't seen before, and about whom they knew nothing.

When the photo of one of the candidates was doctored to make him (the candidates were all male) look more like the person viewing the photos, no matter whether the viewer was male or female, that candidate was judged to be the better of the two and more likely to be voted for.[135]

Also, we relate more easily, and are more likely to help, people who have similar backgrounds and associations. People with camper vans relate to others with camper vans. People from the same area, or with the same background experience such as having been in the armed services, relate to one another easier. Even small similarities like a first name, a shared birthday, or (quite bizarrely) fingerprint similarities, cause people to be more willing to respond positively to a request.[136]

Consistency

This is about what is known as *cognitive dissonance* – the tendency for you to attempt to achieve consistency between your actions and your beliefs. For instance, if you need to buy a car there are a number of choices and you're not sure you'll get the best vehicle or deal. However, once you make the decision you will work to convince yourself that you made the right one and you will behave consistently with that, talking about the car's good features, how good a deal it was, recommending it to friends, etc.

In other words, you work to reduce the dissonance between your action to purchase it and your opinion it was the best deal.

The principle was graphically illustrated by research done with people betting at a racetrack.[137] Bettors about to make a bet stated they felt the horse had "a fair chance of winning". But after having made the bet they said they believed it had "a *good* chance of winning". They needed to reinforce to themselves that their decision was right, so they acted consistently with that.

There is a strong need in people to behave, and appear to behave, consistently with their view of themselves. If you see yourself as a conscientious person, then you are more likely to do the best job you can when asked. If you see yourself as an active person, then you're more likely to join a gym or engage in regular exercise.

You can influence people to behave in a certain way by presenting them with an image of themselves that is complimentary. For instance, if someone does something for you and you thank them by saying, "Thank you, you're a really helpful person", you've just primed them to help you when you ask again. Once they believe they are seen as being a helpful person, they need to continue to give help in order to be consistent with that self-perception.

Commitment

Getting someone to make a commitment is a very powerful influencer of behaviour. A restaurant owner we know says that when she answers a call asking for a reservation, the no-show rate drops dramatically if she asks, "Would you please call and let us know if you are going to cancel". Simply by saying yes to that request the caller has made a commitment.

A research study of 2,416 hotel guests showed that when they made a small but specific commitment to do something like re-using towels and were given a lapel pin to symbolise that commitment, the total number of towels hung for re-use increased by 40%.[138]

If you get someone to make a *written* commitment, or a commitment in public, the compulsion to fulfil it becomes even more powerful. You don't have to ask for a huge commitment. At work you might ask someone to simply initial a report or memo you've written. That signifies agreement to the content, and more importantly, a written commitment to it.

Compliments

We all feel good when we're told something complimentary – "good work", "smart idea", "nice jacket", etc. Don't make the mistake of thinking that hollow compliments are ignored; we also like being complimented even when the compliment is not deserved.

A research study where subjects got either all positive comments, all negative comments, or a mixture of the two produced the unsurprising conclusion that the people who had got only positive compliments liked the appraiser more. But what was surprising is that this happened even when the compliments were recognized by the people being complimented as being quite clearly untrue.[139]

Complimenting people you work with has a strong connection to job success. It sounds cynical, but it's a researched fact that people who make the boss feel good about the decisions he or she has made, and who build up the boss's confidence, tend to do better.[140] And it's not just the boss that you need to pay attention to. Being complimentary about the people you work with makes them more helpful and supportive of you.

If there is someone who you see as an opponent and you speak positively about them and praise them, other people will support you more and trust you more. If you speak negatively about the person, you will be trusted less and get less support from others.[141]

If you're going to compliment someone, be sincere about it, and don't be half-hearted or critical. Backhanded compliments – saying something that at first sounds complimentary but makes a comparison that turns it into a negative – make both the recipient of the comment and observers of your action think negatively of you. And it makes them less interested and motivated to work with you.[142]

Scarcity

Sales and marketing people all understand the power of scarcity. Hence the tag lines for the sale of products like "limited time offer", "limited edition", "until stocks last", "ending Tuesday", and so on. Rarity has value.[143] When what used to be relatively abundant all of a sudden becomes quite scarce, its value increases.[144]

An example is when something ceases to be produced. Automobiles are a depreciating asset. As you drive away from the dealer in your new vehicle its value drops by about a third. But not if you bought a Land Rover Defender just before it went out of production at the end of January 2016. There was no difference between the vehicle on the day before it was announced that production would end, and the day after the announcement, except the perception of sudden scarcity. The value of the vehicle increased sharply.

One of the ways scarcity can relate to you in a job is if you develop a specific skill or knowledge that is to some degree unique and therefore scarce. That's why sales people guard their relationships with good customers so closely. The idea is that if they leave the company they take their customers with them. Nobody else has that relationship with those customers and that makes the sales person rare.

Asking for help and advice

There is a general reluctance to ask people for help. But that is a mistake. The interesting psychological fact is that if you ask someone for their advice or help, they don't just give it and move on, *they feel a responsibility for the success of their advice and they will work to help you achieve it.* When people provide advice, the action puts them into a "merging state of mind" – they feel part of the situation and have a sense of ownership over the consequences. Once they've given the advice they will do what they can to help you succeed.[145]

When you think of asking someone for help, you tend to underestimate the likelihood that they will agree to give it by as much as 50 percent.[146] That's because we don't recognize the difficulty that people have in refusing. Being asked for advice makes people feel knowledgeable and important and they don't want their advice to be a failure. They prefer to be seen as generous and thoughtful, and, to varying degrees, feel a sense of guilt about refusing a request for help. We underestimate the social "cost of saying no" and overestimate the cost of saying "yes".

Research also shows that individuals who make a habit of asking for advice or help from knowledgeable others receive higher performance evaluations than those who never do so.[147] In some sense, being asked for help is flattering and you know what flattery does.

Start with a small request, and if they agree and are flattered by the request, you will be able to build from there. Once someone has agreed to a small request they are more likely to comply with a larger request.[148]

Given that your boss, or bosses, have a significant influence over your success, and given that you are doing work that helps them succeed, make sure you ask, and keep asking "What can I do to make things easier for you?" If you were the boss what would you think about someone who asked you that – and meant it? Not surprisingly, research shows that when that happens the boss is likely to spend more time with you and to develop a close relationship with you.[149]

What Successful People Do

Colin Patey
International Health Care CEO

Colin Patey has run hospitals in Canada, the UK, the Middle East, and the Caribbean. He is a master at change and influencing people to perform at their best. He does it in a warm way that makes everyone comfortable and willing to work together.

This is a brief story of just one instance. In this case it was where he was able to turn around a mental hospital that was ranked among the poorest in the country. It demonstrates his subtle use of all the elements (shown in brackets) that have an influence on people.

On his first day as the new CEO of the hospital, Colin arrived to find a large group of union members picketing the entrance and announcing their intention to go on strike to protest his hiring. So he stopped his car and got out (*got noticed* – all other cars had continued on) and started talking with them. He wasn't driving a fancy car or wearing a fancy suit and they didn't know who he was. Their impression was of someone like them (*similarity*), interested in finding out about them and their grievances.

After he'd listened to what they were concerned about for a little while – essentially that some "outsider bigshot" was coming to cut costs and get rid of people – he told them that actually he was the new CEO, and he invited a group of them to come in to the hospital with him and have some coffee (*warmth*) so he could listen further to their concerns and get their thoughts and advice (*asking for advice or help*).

Having been given a friendly meeting and coffee with the new CEO generated a feeling in the group to reciprocate the kindness; he had listened to them and they were willing to listen to him. Colin suggested that they create a group who would regularly meet with him to discuss changes in the hospital that would benefit all parties. He thanked them for being such open and considerate people (*priming*) and said how much he looked forward to working together with them.

Within two years the hospital was ranked in the top band of mental hospitals in the country.

Key points from this chapter:

- ➤ You influence things by what you do. People see what you do. And they hear what you say. Everything you do has an influence.

- ➤ In order to have influence you need to be noticed.

- ➤ You need to project confidence.

- ➤ Research shows that when you feel powerless you perform poorly, but when you feel you have some control over what's going on, you perform better.

The major ways to create influence:

- ➤ **Reciprocation**: The most powerful influencing factor is reciprocation. Simply giving someone even some small thing, or doing some small thing for them, hugely increases the likelihood of them doing you a favour in return, whether they like you or not.

- ➤ **Contrast**: when you see two things that are different, one after the other, you tend to see the second one as more different than it actually is. If you want someone to do something, begin by asking for something big, then concede that it's not possible and ask for something smaller.

- ➤ **Conformity**: If you want someone to agree to something or do something, it's helpful if you can show it's what others have done or are doing.

- ➤ **Similarity**: People relate more easily with others who have similar backgrounds and associations. Even small similarities like a first name or a shared birthday cause people to be more likely to comply with a request.

- ➤ **Consistency**: If you see yourself as a conscientious person, then you are more likely to do the best job you can when asked. If you see yourself as an active person, then you're more likely to join a gym.

- ➤ **Commitment**: Getting someone to make a commitment is a very powerful influencer. If you get someone to make a *written* commitment, or a commitment in public, the compulsion to fulfil it becomes even more powerful.

- ➤ **Compliments**: Complimenting people who you work with has a strong connection to job success. People who make the boss feel good about the decisions he or she has made, and who build up the boss's confidence, tend to do better.

- ➤ **Scarcity**: If you can develop a skill or knowledge that is somehow unique or scarce you become more valuable and influential.

- ➤ **Asking for help or advice**: if you ask someone for their advice or help, they don't just give it and move on, they feel a responsibility for the success of their advice and they will work to help you achieve it.

Chapter 4

The unconscious influencers

You don't perceive objects as they are.
*You perceive them as **you** are.*
David Eagleman

Managing people's impressions of you

Non-verbal communication

Your actions affect your success because people *see* your actions, even the small involuntary ones that you're not consciously aware of. But a lot, in fact the majority, of the things you do are subconscious. While you may not be aware of them, they're picked up by others, also to a large extent subconsciously.

This is what's called non-verbal communication. You communicate messages non-verbally with things like facial expression, body movement, and posture. You also do it through things like the tone of your voice, your choice of words, and the different emphasis you put on words.

> ➤ Non-verbal behaviour has a much stronger effect in communication than words, either spoken or written.

➢ Non-verbal cues have more than *four times* the effect of spoken words.[150]

➢ Making direct eye contact, rather than not looking straight at someone, causes them to rate you higher on credibility.[151]

➢ Facial expressiveness of public speakers makes them more persuasive, and their audience rates them higher in competence.[152]

➢ A happy expression, with the corners of the mouth turned up and eyebrows relaxed makes you look more trustworthy.[153]

➢ Perhaps the most critical moment when your actions, verbal and nonverbal, have an effect on people is when you first meet them. They form impressions and make judgements about you within the first 11 milliseconds of seeing you.[154]

➢ Observation of someone's behaviour for as little as 30 seconds results in judgements that are as accurate as five minutes of observation.[155]

So what can you do to manage the impression others have of you? If you can pick up clues from their actions and act in ways that either reinforce their favourable impression, or act differently from what they expect if their initial impression is unfavourable, you can help things go your way.

➢ *Two things, warmth and competence, account for more than 90% of the impression, either positive or negative, that people have of you.*[156]

Show warmth first because the brain picks up on warmth faster than competence.[157] While warmth is the more important of the two, you need to exhibit both. Confidence and a feeling of control, as we said earlier, make you act and look more competent. If you also smile, that shows warmth. [158]

When you meet someone, or are talking to someone, here are some things you can do to create a favorable impression:

> ➢ Use the person's name at the start.

> ➢ Look at the person about 60% of the time. Don't stare at them the whole time and don't do things like look at them over the top of your glasses.

> ➢ Don't just look at a person's face, take in their complete body posture and movements. You will get a more accurate reading of their emotions.[159]

> ➢ When the other person is talking, nod and indicate you're listening by saying things like, "Yes", or "Uh huh" or even "um".

> ➢ Lean forward (the "I'm interested position") when you're listening.

> ➢ If you want to appear thoughtful and attentive, tilt your head slightly to one side.

> ➢ Lower the pitch of your voice. Lower pitched voices are perceived to demonstrate more power and leadership.[160] And as we said earlier, it gets people to move towards you and pay more attention.

➤ If you want to appear assured, as you approach another other person or group, think of a situation or event that made you feel successful and confident and keep that in mind.

➤ Try to be aware of, and stop, various nervous gestures like rubbing your hands together or playing with jewellery, etc. Stay still and calm.

➤ Don't rub the back of your neck and look down, which signals doubt or boredom or disbelief.

➤ Don't stay standing while the other person is seated. That will make you appear aggressive and dominant.

➤ Don't slouch or sit in a slumped position. It makes you feel less optimistic and more of a loser, and others read that. Your body posture sends a very strong message.

➤ If you're angry or upset, make sure you get the annoyance out of your mind before you interact with someone. If you don't, they will trust you less.[161]

➤ And here's one that may amuse you, but it's important: wear clothes that are comfortable and not tight or constraining because they allow you to stretch out both physically and mentally and that increases your feeling of being in control. [162]

And here's a really important one:

➤ *Stop thinking about what you're going to say next and waiting for a break in the conversation to say it.*

Listen to the other person! Show interest by asking them to tell you more about what they've been saying. They will like you more and be more willing to continue to interact with you.[163] Remember, people are far less interested in you than they are in themselves.

But when you create a good first impression you also need to understand what sustains that impression, and what you can do about it. Once people have formed an impression, they tend to discount things that run counter to that, and in addition they act in ways that help to prove their initial opinion correct. That works whether their first impression was positive or negative. This makes it doubly important to try to create a good impressing to begin with. If you get off on the wrong foot it takes a lot of effort to set things right, and sometimes it's just not possible.

Mirroring – a special aspect of non-verbal behaviour

You can change the behaviour of someone else by the way you behave. If you smile and exude warmth the other person finds it difficult not to reciprocate. If you're grumpy and gruff, you tend to get the same behaviour in return. This phenomenon is called *mirroring*.

When your brain registers even the minutest expression of an emotion (and that occurs at a subconscious level) – a slight smile, a frown, a narrowing of the eyes, a slight downturn of the mouth – even though the expression may be fleeting, a very interesting thing happens.

Your own facial muscles move to mirror that movement.[164] The brain has what are called "mirror neurons" that mentally copy the actions that you observe.[165] This mental mimicking enables you to understand other people better. And it gets them to understand you better.

The process is driven by the amygdala, the part of the brain that developed in the early stages of our existence. It's responsible for processing strong emotions, and is particularly sensitive to fear.[166] It picks up the tiniest clues from people's expressions, posture and movements and dictates your reaction to them. Most of the time you are completely unaware of these reactions.

Here's an example of this. You're looking for something – a shop or the nearest bus stop or the location of an office, or whatever – and you approach the person or people sitting behind a desk with a sign "Information" or "Reception" to ask a question. We've all had the experience; sometimes the person behind the desk is very helpful, even going out of their way to help you find what you're looking for, and sometimes they're "busy" and either don't help or help minimally. What makes the difference? You'll say it's the mood of the person behind the desk, and that's part of it. But it's possible for you to change that mood, perhaps not 100% of the time, but a lot of the time.

By mirroring you create an emotional connection with the other party, either reinforcing positive emotions or negative ones.[167] So when you approach the person behind the desk with a smile, or even a slight, unconscious friendly gesture, they get the message and tend to mirror it, initiating a move towards a positive relationship.

Then when you ask for help, you will have greatly raised the probability of a positive response.

But it's no use trying to act as though you're being friendly when actually you're mad as hell, or frustrated, or upset, because these emotions will be picked up by the other person.

The botox effect – cracking the mirror

As you know, botox injections alter the expression and movement in an individual's face. The scientific explanation of how that works is that botox blocks the movement of a neurotransmitter that sends signals from the brain to the facial muscles. These signals tell the muscles when to flex and move, but when they can't get the message, the muscles stay relaxed.

Botox may erase wrinkles and make you look younger, but it has a rather big downside and that's because the emotions of people who've had botox treatment become masked. Their faces don't show their emotions clearly and that means you can't read them correctly. And because you can't read their emotional signals properly, you can't mirror them properly. You don't understand what they're feeling or communicating. But making the interaction even more difficult, *they* can't read *you* because you aren't mirroring what they're feeling.

To make matters even worse, when a person's facial mobility is impaired, their overall judgement of emotional signals, even in *pictures* of faces, is poor.[168].
As a result, because it's difficult for them to mirror what they are seeing in your face, you see them as less likeable. Your brain works out what can be trusted and what can't, and the message it sends is that if it can't read normal signals, it can't trust what you're seeing.

Your influence on you: your actions and their effect on you

We told you at the start of the book that if you squeezed a soft rubber ball in your right hand for a few minutes you would feel more positive and feel up for a challenge. That was just one example of the fact that *physical actions have a direct effect on feelings and emotions*. We tend to believe that feelings and emotions drive actions, but it also works the other way.

We all try to manage the impressions we give to others.[169] How you present yourself to other people affects not just the way they see you, but also *the way you see yourself*. And that, in turn, affects how you subsequently act.[170]

The actions you take determine your subsequent behaviour and your view of yourself.

> ➤ If you're going into a situation where you're feeling nervous and unsure, before you go in, stand for a couple of minutes in what's known as a "power pose" – head up, chin forward a bit, shoulders set, arms relaxed at your side, not spread wide but not tight to your body. This creates an "experience" and causes an actual physical change in your brain that makes you feel more comfortable and more confident.[171]

> ➤ Hold your fist clenched for a minute or two. That will make you feel more assertive.[172] (By the way, that's one of the reasons why athletes do a clenched fist pump; it raises their testosterone levels.)

> ➤ While you're doing a task at your desk, if you sit up straight rather than in a slumped position, you will

feel more positive about what you're doing and what you've accomplished.[173]

➢ Gesture with your hands when you're trying to make a point or you're making a presentation. Moving your hands activates an area in the brain called Broca's area which is important for speech formation. Hand movement helps you clarify your thinking and verbal expression.[174]

➢ If you hold a pencil between your clenched teeth it forces your lips into an artificial smile and you will feel happier.[175]

➢ If you hold a small object between your eyebrows, it furrows your brow into an artificial scowl, and you will feel in a bad mood. [176]

➢ Simply looking at a picture of a happy face, or an emoji of a happy face, causes the muscles around your mouth to, at least momentarily, contract upwards in a smile.[177]

➢ Smiling is contagious.[178] While smiling makes you feel happier, being contagious, it puts people around you in a better mood.

➢ An unfortunate fact is that 14% of people smile less than five times a day.[179] But smiling has been shown to be positively correlated with longevity – the more you smile the greater your chances of living longer.[180]

➢ Facial expressions affect how emotions are registered in the brain. If you put your hand into ice water and smile while you hold it there, you'll be able to do it for longer, and you will get over the pain faster than if you don't smile.[181]

Things do work the other way of course, and your brain affects what your body does. For instance, when the left side of your brain is active, your attention goes to the right. [182]. A somewhat off-beat demonstration of this is that when soccer goalkeepers are behind in a penalty shootout the pressure to perform activates their left brain and that gets them to dive to the right seven times out of ten.[183]

The effect of "outside" things that influence others – and you

While you influence other people by what you do, and they influence you in a similar fashion, there are also external things that affect your perception and behaviour. These "outside" influences act on your subconscious and create a mood or emotion.[184] It's what we talked about earlier, *priming*, only this time it's not about being primed by what someone says about you, it's an external influence.

Things that are happening around you, or in the background, have an effect on your thoughts and actions. The eminent social and cognitive psychologist, John Bargh, says, "conscious experiences in one situation linger into the next situation without our realizing it and become the unconscious influences in that subsequent setting".[185]

Priming is a subconscious effect where a context of some sort triggers a memory that "primes" an action. For instance, an experience everyone has had is passing a bakery or coffee shop and getting the aromas, and all of sudden feeling like having a coffee or a bun. You're reminded of how delicious buns and breads and cakes and coffees, etc. are, and that memory primes you to want to have some.

Here are some examples of external things affecting you emotions and actions:

> If you're holding a warm cup of coffee, you see other people as emotionally warmer.[186] And the reverse is true; holding something cold makes you see others as colder emotionally.

> Feeling cold makes you less trusting of others. [187]

> If you're made to feel part of, and involved in a group – family, friends, workmates – you will feel physically warmer. If you feel rejected, you'll feel colder.[188]

> If you're sitting in a hard chair you will negotiate more strongly, but if you're sitting in a soft chair you will yield more. [189]

> When German songs are played on a wine shop's sound system, customers are more likely to buy a German wine, but if the songs are French they are more likely to buy a French wine.[190]

> Smiling is connected with positive emotions so when someone who is not in any way involved in buying a

product smiles, another person considering buying the product, simply seeing the smile, has a more positive attitude to it.[191]

➢ And here's a bit of advice. Avoid checking the box about age on questionnaires or surveys because it will prime you for a negative stereotype of age.[192]

What Successful People Do

Wanda Sevilla Krieb
Managing Director, Spring Professional

Wanda has had a distinguished career in recruitment and retention and has interviewed more than seven thousand people. Here is some advice she has for young people interviewing for a job.

The job interview

"When you attend a job interview, show your strength and drive to succeed. Be positive. Interviewers are aware that young candidates may have little experience, and you should be aware of this. Trying to pretend you have knowledge and experience when you don't means you will be the first to be dismissed during a selection process."

During the selection process, she says, perception becomes reality. Smiling, being calm, and listening carefully helps you connect. Warmth and competence determine 90% of your first impression.

Be positive. If you arrive to your interview complaining about things, or making excuses about things, this will not help you connect. Being positive helps you connect; being negative does the opposite.

Changing jobs for money

Wanda's advice is, "If you want to change jobs, do it for the right reasons". When you're thinking about a job she recommends you look beyond the amount of money offered. Do some research about the company's work environment. Find out about its reputation; it doesn't help your career to take a job at a company with a bad reputation. Try to find out about the organization's philosophy, and what its vision is. It's obviously better to be with a company that's moving forward than one that lacks vision and drive. Finally, she says, "If they can manage it, I advise candidates to arrange to have a casual breakfast, or an away-from-the-business coffee or something, with their future boss. This will allow them to know more about the boss's philosophy and to discover if there's a good chemistry."

Leaving your job because of your boss

If you find that your relationship with your boss is not going well, Wanda recommends you ask them for an hour of their time to talk about their expectations of you. A great deal of underperformance is due not to lack of effort, but to not understanding what's expected of you and, as a result, doing the wrong things.

Key points from this chapter:

➢ The majority, of the things you do are subconscious.

➢ Non-verbal cues have more than *four times* the effect of spoken words.

➢ Making direct eye contact, rather than not looking directly at someone, causes them to rate you higher on credibility.

➢ A happy expression, with the corners of the mouth turned up and eyebrows relaxed makes you look more trustworthy.

➢ People form impressions and make judgements about you within the first 11 milliseconds of seeing you.

➢ Two things, warmth and competence, account for more than 90% of the impression, either positive or negative, that people have of you. Show warmth first because the brain picks up on warmth faster than competence.

➢ When you meet someone, or are talking to someone, here are some things you can do to create a favorable impression:

> ➢ Use the person's name at the start.

> ➢ Look at the person about 60% of the time. Don't stare at them the whole time and don't

do things like look at them over the top of your glasses.

➤ Don't just look at a person's face, take in their complete body posture and movements. You will get a more accurate reading on their emotions.

➤ When the other person is talking, nod and indicate you're listening by saying things like, "Yes", or "Uh huh" or even "um".

➤ Lean forward (the "I'm interested position") when you're listening.

➤ If you want to appear thoughtful and attentive, look directly at the person you're interacting with 60-70% of the time and tilt your head slightly to one side.

➤ Lower the pitch of your voice. Lower pitched voices are perceived to demonstrate more power and leadership.

➤ If you want to appear assured, as you approach another other person or group, think of a situation or event that made you feel successful and confident and keep that in mind.

➤ Try to be aware of, and stop, various nervous gestures like rubbing your hands or playing with jewellery, etc. Stay still and calm.

- Don't rub the back of your neck and look down, which signals doubt or boredom or disbelief.

- Don't stay standing while the other person is seated. That will make you appear aggressive and dominant.

- *Stop thinking about what you're going to say next and listen to the other person!* Show interest by asking them to tell you more about what they've been saying. They will like you more and be more willing to continue to interact with you. Remember, people are far less interested in you than they are in themselves.

- Mirroring. You can change the behaviour of someone else by the way you behave. If you smile and exude warmth the other person finds it difficult not to reciprocate. If you're grumpy and gruff, you tend to get the same behaviour in return.

- People who've had botox treatment don't show their emotions clearly and that means you can't read them correctly.

- Things that are happening around you, or in the background have an effect on your thoughts and actions.

- Gesture with your hands when you're trying to make a point or you're making a presentation. Hand movement helps you clarify your thinking and verbal expression.

Chapter 5

Handling pressure and stress

There is always stress, so the only thing is to make sure that it is useful to yourself and others
Hans Selye

There are two sides to stress; it can be good or it can be bad. That very much depends on you.

We know what you're thinking: "What sort of stupid statement is that? Everyone knows it's bad, and never good. Just look at the statistics". But remember the old saying, "There are lies, damned lies, and statistics". In this case, the statistics only tell one side of the story. It's a pretty grim side, but there is another story, and this is once again a scientifically proven fact: **stress can make you stronger, smarter, and more successful**.[193]
Stress can be good – if you deal with it properly.

If you deal with it positively and correctly it can have big benefits. For one thing, having a positive view of it makes you live longer. But if you take the opposite position and deal with it negatively and let it run rampant over your emotions, there is only the downside of mental and physical ill health.
How you view stress is a mindset issue. You need to trust the facts and disregard the vast amount of nonsense that is published every day in newspapers, magazines, and on-line social media. These are the facts about stress:

- It can improve your productivity and performance [194]

- It can improve your health and make you stronger [195]

- It can accelerate your learning and make you smarter [196]

If you believe these facts about stress, and not the negative garbage that's designed to make you feel disadvantaged, picked on, and needing help (which, coincidentally, will cost you money, so the "helpers" are not completely altruistic)), research shows that: [197]

- You will be more satisfied

- You will be less depressed

- You will have fewer health problems

- You will have more energy

- You will be happier at work and home

- You will be more confident about rising to challenges successfully

Some of the chemistry of stress

Stress doesn't just release cortisol (the so-called "stress hormone") into the system, it also releases a hormone called DHEA.

DHEA is a steroid. We think of steroids as the things that athletes take to get accelerated muscle growth from exercise. DHEA does something similar but it's a *neuro*steroid – it accelerates *brain* growth when you have stressful experiences. And DHEA works against the action of cortisol.[198]

> ➤ The key is the balance between DHEA and cortisol. That balance is called *The Growth Index*. The higher the index – i.e. the more DHEA relative to cortisol – the greater the positive effects such as:
>
>> ▪ better problem-solving skills [199]
>> ▪ greater persistence and resilience [200]
>> ▪ better focus [201]

> ➤ If you look at potentially stressful situations as a challenge and a positive learning opportunity, rather than a threat, you increase your Growth Index.

> ➤ Having a positive view of stress gives you strength, makes you more alert, and makes the brain process what's going on quicker.

> ➤ Stress can be used to focus attention and concentration. Think of top level golfers addressing a crucial shot, or tennis players facing a crucial point. They take the stress of the situation and use it to sharpen their concentration. They see the situation as a challenge, not a threat.

> ➤ A moderate level of stress and adversity makes you stronger, more resilient, healthier and happier.[202]

➢ Stress can also give you a motivational boost because it stimulates the release of a cocktail of hormones – dopamine, adrenaline, testosterone, endorphins – that give you a rush and make you feel more powerful and confident. At the extreme, this is the sort of reaction that skydivers get.[203]

➢ Stress can make you more trusting of others and can improve your emotional quotient (EQ).[204]

If you're really committed to achieving job success you can't avoid stress. It's part of work life and life in general. For instance, simply living in an urban environment makes you more sensitive to social stress.[205]

➢ Don't try to, as many people do, avoid stress by doing things like trying to distract yourself. [206] That is precisely the wrong thing to do.

➢ Spending time and energy avoiding stress makes you feel less happy, less satisfied, and generally less pleased with things.[207]

➢ Attempts at avoidance also cause you to become depressed.[208]

Stress is contagious

Unfortunately, stress is contagious.[209] When people are feeling stressed, they "transmit" those feelings to others, and even infants pick them up.

An experiment to demonstrate this separated mothers from their babies and took one group of mothers and put them through a stressful experience while a second group of mothers did something pleasant and unthreatening.

When the stressed mothers were returned to their babies, the babies immediately picked up their feeling of stress and mirrored their feelings, while the babies with the unstressed mothers reacted calmly.[210]

How you engage and manage stress, and what your expectations are – learning vs. failure, challenge vs. acceptance, focus vs. panic, strength vs. defeat – makes a difference between your success or lack of it.

This is a critically important point. The whole issue about dealing effectively with pressure and stress is summed up in this sentence: *The effect you expect is the effect you get.*

What that means is that, given possible different outcomes of an action, the outcome you most expect tends to become the most likely. No, we're *not* saying you have magical powers. But the fact is that what you believe affects how you react to things. You may find this difficult to believe, but it's proven by extensive research and we'll describe a few examples.

A study of mindset about stress showed one set of subjects a 3-minute video about stress being positive and strengthening, while a second set of subjects saw a 3-minute video about stress being negative and weakening. The subjects were then asked to give a short presentation during which they were constantly harangued with negative, stressful, feedback comments.

Those who had watched the "stress-is-enhancing" video showed fewer stress indicators after being subjected to the negative feedback than the ones who saw the "stress-is-harmful" video.[211] *The effect you expect is the effect you get.*

Another example is the "Shake Testing Study".[212] Subjects of the experiment were asked to fast overnight, and when they appeared the following morning, they were given a milkshake with a label on it saying it contained 620 calories and 30 grams of fat. A week later they were again asked to fast overnight and when they arrived in the morning, they were given a milkshake labelled as having 140 calories and 0 grams of fat.

For both sessions, after the participants had finished the milkshakes, they had blood samples taken. What was being tested was the level of a hormone called ghrelin. It's called the "hunger hormone". When the ghrelin level in your blood goes down you feel full, when it goes up, you feel hungry.

Here's what makes this experiment so interesting: both of the milkshakes, at the first test and the second test, were exactly the same. They both had 380 calories. But when the group thought the shake had 620 calories, they showed a ghrelin drop three times greater – i.e. felt really full – than when they drank the second milkshake, after which their ghrelin level was higher, and they felt hungry.

What they believed about the calorie content of the shakes, and what they expected as a result affected them not just mentally, but *physically. The effect you expect is the effect you get.*

The same effect was demonstrated in an experiment where subjects were given a small histamine skin prick test that caused an allergic skin reaction and then had a physician administer an inert cream with no active ingredients to the affected area.[213] For half of the subjects the physician acted with warmth and competence and assured them that the cream would reduce the irritation. For the other half of the subjects, the physician acted coldly and less competently and told them the cream was likely to increase the reaction. You guessed it: the rash diminished for the ones who were told it would do so by someone they saw as competent and caring, but it didn't for the others. *The effect you expect is the effect you get.*

Two studies on beliefs about aging tell the same story. One study tracked individuals, ranging in age from 18 to 49, for 38 years, and found that those people who had positive views of old people (wise, interesting, cheerful, agreeable) had an 80% lower risk of heart attack than those who held negative views (useless, irritable, unpleasant, etc.).[214] Another study showed that people who had positive views about aging recovered from heart attacks quicker.[215] *The effect you expect is the effect you get.*

Dealing with pressure and stress

The first thing to recognize is that you aren't completely powerless. You do have some control over your life.

You need to understand and believe that, because if you believe it you will see stress more as a challenge than a threat, and as we've pointed out, that has a major effect on your health and chances of longevity.

When people who believe they have some control of their lives and behaviour face stress their brains produce far less of the hormone cortisol than the brains of people who don't think they have any control.[216]

Hold onto your seat because here's a simple and easy way to reduce stress:

> ➢ Before you begin something that you think will be stressful, say out loud, "I am excited" several times.

> Do you find it hard to believe that works? An experiment at the University of Pennsylvania proves that it does. It put subjects through three stressful situations – singing karaoke in front of an audience of strangers, making a public speech, and solving difficult mathematical problems under time pressure. Before each of these tasks, subjects were told to say out loud either "I am excited", or "I am anxious", or "I am calm".

Here's what the study found, and this is bulletproof fact! People who spoke the words "I am excited" performed better on all the tasks. [217]

> Simply saying "I am excited" out loud makes you feel more self-confident and gets you to perform better. Saying "I feel anxious" has the completely opposite effect. Saying "I feel calm" has no effect. So when you're stressed or anxious, trying to calm yourself is not the thing to do. You need to see the situation as a challenge that you are excited to engage and overcome. Remember, "I am excited!"

How to change the way you think about pressure and stress

As we've shown, how you think about stress determines its effect on you. If you take a positive view and see it as a challenge and a positive learning opportunity, you increase your Growth Index and you become stronger, smarter and more competent. If you take a negative view, you become anxious, depressed, and less healthy, let alone also shortening your life.

Here are six steps you can take to change your view about stress from a negative one to a positive one:

1. **Recognize and acknowledge stress when you experience it.** Don't try to avoid it, or pretend it's not happening to you, or try to divert your attention from it. That makes you feel unhappy, unsatisfied and less pleased with things. Pressure and stress are real and there is no quick "escape". Drink or drugs just mask the facts, they don't remove them.

2. **Ask yourself why you're feeling stressed.** What's the cause? Can you deal with it? If you can remove the cause you will remove the reaction. It can be as simple as being stressed about getting to work or meetings on time. The solution may be to start earlier.

3. Before you get too bogged down and emotional about something, **ask yourself if it's something you really care about?** Will the outcome change your life in some way? Or is it something that in the long term really doesn't make much difference?

4. **View pressure and stress as a challenge** and use the energy that gives you to think of how you can deal with it. Look at it as a learning experience and think about not just how to deal with it now, but how to ensure it doesn't get to you again, or have the same effect.

5. **If you can't get rid of the cause, then change the way you react to it.** You can control your emotions and behaviour.

And there's a final step:

6. **If it's your boss who's the cause of the stress, don't try to confront her or him, at least not alone.** Christine Porath says that she has found that 85% of individuals who choose confrontation with an uncivil boss make things worse.[218] But that depends on whether you decide to go alone or with a united group. A research study found that when employees banded together to confront the individual, none of them were fired and 58% of the offenders were punished. But when individuals took on their abusers alone only 27% of the offenders were punished and 20% of the accusers were fired.[219]

What Successful People Do

Rodrigo Azpurua
CEO, Riviera Point Development Group

The property development business by its nature involves continuing uncertainty. In every project things occur that can't be foreseen and controlled for. It's not something that you can avoid completely.

Therefore, if you are to be successful, you need to have a clear strategy and approach for dealing with stress. Rodrigo says that when unexpected and stressful things occur it's important to take a positive approach and ask yourself, "What are the action options? What changes do I need to make?"

In 2007 when the bottom fell out of the development and construction industry, Rodrigo says the lesson he learned changed his approach to crisis and stress.

"During the crisis", he says, "I stopped blaming myself for my mistakes because it did me no good. However, when I thought about my options for the future, I found positive things. For instance, I needed a healthy body and mind so I started exercise routines in a disciplined way as well as deep spiritual work."

Experience backs up what the research says about having positive people around you when things get stressful and difficult. Rodrigo says, "Life has made me become very selective when it comes to the people I want to work with."

He says one of the keys to his personal success has been making sure he is surrounded by positive people.

He makes an effort to steer clear of individuals who lack a high level of self-consciousness and are not aware of their weaknesses. "When things go wrong and this type of person is under pressure", he says, "they project their frustration and negative sentiment onto the people around them".

> ➤ His advice is for people to learn the real facts about stress: that it can improve your productivity and performance;

> ➤ that it can improve your health and make you stronger;

> ➤ that it can accelerate your learning and make you smarter;
> and

> ➤ that if you take a positive approach to it, you'll be healthier and be likely to live longer.

Key points from this chapter:

➢ Stress can make you stronger, smarter, and more successful

➢ The actual facts about stress:

    ➢ It can improve your productivity and performance

    ➢ It can improve your health and make you stronger

    ➢ It can accelerate your learning and make you smarter

    ➢ If you view it positively you are likely to live longer

➢ The results pf a positive attitude to stress:

    ➢ You will be more satisfied

    ➢ You will be less depressed

    ➢ You will have fewer health problems

    ➢ You will have more energy

    ➢ You will be happier at work and home

    ➢ You will be more confident about rising to challenges successfully

➢ As well as triggering cortisol, stressful experiences release the neurosteroid DHEA which accelerates brain growth.

➢ The key is the balance between DHEA and cortisol. That balance is called *The Growth Index*. The higher the index – i.e. the more DHEA relative to cortisol – the greater the positive effects such as:

> ➢ better problem-solving skills,
>
> ➢ greater persistence and resilience
>
> ➢ better focus

➢ If you look at potentially stressful situations as a challenge and a positive learning opportunity, rather than a threat, you increase your Growth Index.

➢ Don't try to avoid stress by doing things like trying to distract yourself. Spending time and energy avoiding stress makes you feel less happy, less satisfied, and generally less pleased with things.

➢ Attempts at avoidance also cause you to become depressed.

➢ Stress is contagious. Your transmit it and sense it in others subconsciously.

➢ The effect you expect is the effect you get. Remember the Shake Testing Study.

➢ Before you begin something that you think will be stressful, say out loud, "I am excited" several times.

➢ Six steps you can take to change your view about stress from a negative one to a positive one:

1. Recognize and acknowledge stress when you experience it. Don't try to avoid it, or pretend it's not happening to you, or try to divert your attention from it. That makes you feel unhappy, unsatisfied and less pleased with things. Pressure and stress are real and there is no quick "escape". Drink or drugs just mask the facts, they don't remove them.

2. Ask yourself why you're feeling stressed. What's the cause? Can you deal with it? If you can remove the cause you will remove the reaction. It can be as simple as being stressed about getting to work or meetings on time. The solution is start earlier.

3. Before you get too bogged down and emotional about something, ask yourself if it's something you really care about? Will the outcome change your life in some way? Or is it something that in the long term really doesn't make much difference?

4. View pressure and stress as a challenge and use the energy that gives you to think of how you can deal with it. Look at it as a learning experience

and think about not just how to deal with it now, but how to ensure it doesn't get to you again, or have the same effect.

5. If you can't get rid of the cause, then change the way you react to it.

6. If it's your boss who's the cause of the stress, don't try to confront her or him, at least not alone.

Chapter 6

The causes of stress and your reactions to it

The greatest weapon against stress is our ability to choose one thought over another
William James

It helps if you know what's causing you stress, because if you know the cause and you can deal with it, the stress will go away. But the reality is that sometimes the cause is too overpowering and too far beyond your ability to control. When that happens we use the word "toxic".

It's an overused term, and in the popular media is used for anything that's felt to be unpleasant, and because it's applied to relatively mild things it becomes seen as a less threatening and dangerous thing. But the traditional meaning of toxic is "poisonous", so when we talk here about toxic workplaces and toxic work, we're talking about the real, basic meaning of the word: things that have a seriously harmful (poisonous) physical and/or mental effect on you.

Toxic workplaces and Toxic work

You may be able to deal with moderate doses of poison but some workplaces and some jobs cannot be handled, no matter how positive your view of stress. They are truly lethal, and the only thing to do is get away from them and stay away.

Jobs are the number one reported cause of stress.[220] People in general don't have an aversion to work; they happily engage in all sorts of activities. Jobs can be enjoyable, rewarding, fulfilling, and at times just plain fun. When that's the case there isn't any stress involved, but obviously there must be a lot of toxic jobs to cause these statistics:

> In Britain 85% of people say they feel stressed regularly [221]

> Half of these people say that they are worried about the effect that stress has on their health

> In Canada 23% of people below age 35, and 30% of those between 35 and 54, say that most days they feel "quite a bit" or "extremely" stressed [222]

> In a large survey in the US, 45% of people reported lying awake at night and suffering regular sleeplessness due to stress. [223]

> In Britain, the Health and Safety Executive says that in 2015/16, stress accounted for 37% of all work-related ill health cases and 45% of all working days lost due to ill health.

> And it says that 11.7 million working days were lost due to stress over that period.[224]

> Researchers investigating the costs of stress to business in the United States estimate it accounts for approximately 5-8% of annual healthcare costs.[225] *Forbes* estimates the cost in dollar terms as being as high as $190 billion.

Working in a toxic environment has a huge cost.

➤ Toxic workplaces and toxic work result in an increased probability of

> ➤ cancer [226]

> ➤ heart attack [227]

> ➤ stroke [228]

> ➤ deteriorating mental health [229]

> ➤ suicide [230]

➤ At a lower but still harmful level they cause headaches, muscle aches, upset stomach, insomnia, loss of sexual desire and/or ability, and frequent colds or infections.[231]

➤ They are as bad for women's health as smoking and obesity.[232]

➤ Toxic workplaces are the 5th leading cause of death in the USA – 120,000 excess deaths per year.[233]

➤ Worldwide research almost 20 years ago into the effects of toxic workplaces estimated 850,000 excess deaths and the loss of 24 million years of life.[234] The numbers are likely to be much higher now.

> If you're currently working in a really toxic environment, our urgent advice is *"Get out!"* And do it as soon as you can. The sooner the better. The longer you remain in an abusive, toxic environment, the more you will suffer long-lasting emotional damage.[235]

> But a word of advice: If you are leaving a job, always try to leave on good terms. Never bad mouth your employer.

> If you have done that to your former boss or company, even though what you said may have been true, people who might be thinking of hiring you will wonder if you might do the same to them.

> Don't make a scene or vent your anger or frustration when you leave. It may make you feel better at the time but it can do lasting damage. The last impression people have of you is the one they remember. And if you're asked to an exit interview, don't unload a lot of criticism; say a lot more positive things than negatives.

> Try not to quit without another job to go to. The best time to look for another job is when you already have one.

People stay in toxic workplaces for a number of reasons, one of which, of course, is economic. Unless you're independently wealthy you need a job to live.

But there are a number of other factors that help you rationalise not leaving. One of these is the pretty universal need to think well of yourself.[236] You stay because don't want to think of yourself as a quitter, or that you're not strong enough to take the pressure, or you don't want to admit you made a bad decision to take the job in the first place.

Another reason is social influence – if everyone else seems to be handling the situation and thinks it's OK, then you convince yourself it must be. And a third is effort justification. The more work and effort and energy you put into something, and the more you endure the difficulty and hardships involved, the more you value something.[237]

Try not to fall into those traps. Take a step back and look at the effects the job is having on you. No matter how much a job pays, or how prestigious it is, the negative effects on your health far outweigh any of those things.

What causes stress?

The dictionary definition of stress is "A state of mental or emotional strain or tension resulting from adverse or demanding circumstances". But Dr. Kelly McGonigal has a much more useful definition. She says stress is *"what arises when something you care about is at stake"*.[238] Think about it; you don't get stressed by things you don't care about.

Four major stressors that you care about and that you're likely to experience over your work life are:

> Lack of control

> Unpredictability

> Rejection

> Threats to your self-esteem

Lack of control

Large organizations are hierarchical and the lower you are in the hierarchy, the less control you have and the more you feel the effects of pressure and stress.

> A large research study showed that the lower a person's job level, the higher the probability of them experiencing heart disease or death.[239] The research found that job control was the single most important predictor of heart disease for people in the organization.

> A study of more than 600 people in 70+ organizations showed that the lower the level of control they had in their jobs, the higher their level of depression and anxiety.[240]

> Another study showed that lack of job control led to high levels of anxiety, depression, irritability, sadness and hopelessness.[241]

> But perhaps an even more worrying effect of lack of job control is the phenomenon of learned helplessness. When people have no control over what they do, and no control over what happens to them, they give up and stop making any effort.[242]

At its worst, individuals who feel severe lack of control can finally snap and resort to extreme behaviour. An example is the incidence of multiple fatal shootings at offices of the US postal system (35 killings in 8 incidents between 1986 and 2017) which spawned the phrase "going postal". The fact that these shootings have continued over a period of 30 years doesn't say much for the management in the system.

However, even in the most extreme cases you have some control. What you can control is your reaction to the situation. The neurologist and psychiatrist Viktor Frankl, a Holocaust survivor, was a prisoner first in Auschwitz and then in a camp associated with Dachau. It's difficult to think of more extreme circumstances of loss of control. His advice is, "When we are no longer able to change a situation, we are challenged to change ourselves".[243] You always have control over some things. Look at the situation from a different perspective. Try to focus on the positives. Make fun in your mind of some of the more ridiculous elements, and so on.

Unpredictability/uncertainty

A second major stressor is unpredictability. If you miss your bus and you may be late for work, or you can't find a taxi, what are the chances there will there be another along in the next few minutes?

Or will it be 15 minutes, or 30, or maybe not at all? Unconsciously, you start to figure out the probability of a 5-minute delay. But if your first estimate is wrong, what are the odds your next one, a 15-minute delay, is correct? Should you cut your losses and walk 15 minutes to another bus route or location? But what if, just after you've moved, a bus or taxi appears?

Just reading this you can feel the uncertainty and stress rising. The greater the uncertainty, the more stressful the experience.

If lack of control and uncertainty combine – for instance your boss is all sweetness and light one moment and explodes with rage the next – your level of stress will be even higher.[244]

There are different levels of uncertainty. There's uncertainty about something with major consequences ("Will I lose my job?"), and there's uncertainty about things that don't make much difference ("Will I be a bit late for lunch?").

It's important to put things in perspective. If you miss your bus, what's the worst thing that can happen? Is this really a big deal, or are you just making it one? It's easy to get wound up about something that's really not important. A lot of stress is self-generated.

Rejection and threats to self-esteem

Another stressor is rejection by others, or the fear of rejection. People have a need to be part of something, to "belong", and to have the support of others, and a feeling of belonging is not just something "nice"; it's vitally important for health and wellbeing.[245]

➢ There is a strong correlation between social support and better health.[246] [247]

➢ Social support relieves stress, regulates insulin, strengthens the immune system, and triggers the release of stress-reducing hormones.[248]

➢ Social support also correlates positively with lower rates of cancer.[249]

Social bonding releases the neurohormone oxytocin to the brain. That makes you more sensitive to the feelings and emotions of others, enhances your empathy, and suppresses the fight or flight response because it dampens the fear response. Oxytocin also helps regenerate micro damage to your heart because the heart has special receptors for it.[250]

We use the word "painful" to describe the feeling of rejection. Psychologists call this *social pain*, as opposed to physical pain, and research shows that one of the differences between the two is that once physical pain has gone, it's gone, but social pain can be re-experienced, or "relived".[251]
After it's healed you may remember that a fall or break or burn was painful, but you don't re-experience the actual pain. However, when you remember social pain, the memory reinforces the pain. Mental bullying on social media highlights this problem.

One of the most destructive and damaging things is the "like" button on social media because its positive effects are only short-lived. Only 12.5% of people are able to keep the happy feeling for as long as an hour.[252]

But negative social comparisons – *lack* of likes, or comments that mock you, belittle you, threaten you, and strip you of self-esteem, have a much longer lasting effect and lead to depression and anxiety.[253]

Sean Parker, the founding president of Facebook says that the like button on Facebook is a "social-validation feedback loop" that gives you "a little dopamine hit". *In other words, from the very start, the like button was meant to be, and is, addictive.*

We suggested some ways to combat that addictiveness earlier. You don't *have to* generate lots of "likes" for things. You don't *have to* expose yourself and your life to people you don't know, and never will. Stop putting yourself in situations where there is more downside potential than there is upside!

Self-evaluative threat

Every group has criteria for membership, some of which are central and essential, and others which determine social standing in the group. If you fulfil all the conditions, you remain a member of good and high standing. If you don't fulfil a few of the peripheral ones, you may remain a member, but you're assigned a lower standing.

If you don't meet the core criteria, you are rejected. And that raises the issue of another major stressor, threat to your self-concept and self-esteem. The psychological term is *self-evaluative threat* and it has physical consequences as well as psychological ones.[254] It raises anxiety and heart rate [255] and also causes negative chemical changes in your body.[256]

If you think about it, a lot of the pressure and stress you experience is about threats to your self-image (or as Dr McGonigal phrased it "when something you care about is at stake") – your competence, your likeability, your intelligence, your appearance, your power, your expertise, etc. Research shows that when people's self-concept is threatened, and they are also in situations where they have little or no control over things, the situation is hugely stressful.[257]

When you're faced with one of these types of situations, remember to ask yourself the question, "How much do I *really* care about this? Is this going to have a major effect on my life, or is it something that I would have just liked to happen (or not happen) that really doesn't make a lot of difference?"

Remember from the previous chapter, *the effect you expect is the effect you get.*

> ➤ *Believing that the stress you are experiencing is damaging your health increases your probability of dying early by 43%.*[258]

> ➤ If you see stressful situations as a challenge and a learning experience you will perform better, [259]

> ➤ And you will have more energy, be healthier and more satisfied with life. [260]

The physical and emotional effects of stress

Your brain is hyper-sensitive to you being at the receiving end of negative behaviour. The surge of cortisol that results from being criticised, belittled, bullied, pressured or rejected, especially in public, heightens your focus on the event and makes your memories of it more vivid. While positive experiences trigger the brain to release oxytocin, negative ones release cortisol.

Oxytocin creates a feeling of pleasure, but it disappears from the bloodstream in about five minutes. However, after a stressful event, cortisol lingers for an hour or two.[261] [262] The ill effects of stress take time to fade away, they don't just stop immediately after you leave the situation which triggered them.

Intense or prolonged stress weakens the working of the pre-frontal cortex (PFC) which runs cognitive abilities.
Those abilities are the brain-based skills you need to carry out any task, like how you learn, remember, problem-solve, pay attention, etc. Even quite mild stress over time can cause a significant loss of pre-frontal cognitive abilities.[263] The PFC also drives creativity and imagination and sensible decision-making. Therefore, the longer you allow yourself to feel under stress the greater the damage to your creativity, and to your ability to make good decisions.

Stress triggers activity in the HPA (hypothalamic-pituitary-adrenalin) area of the brain, which activates large bursts of adrenalin, cortisol and pro-inflammatory cytokine. At high levels, these interfere with the way the brain functions, shrinking cells and affecting decision making. For instance:

➤ People who continue to suffer from severe stress have poorer memory.[264]

➤ High stress levels cause people's emotions to become confused.[265]

➤ Prolonged high levels of stress can cause hypertension and heart disease, damage to the immune system, diabetes, depression, and even things like colds and flu.[266]

➤ And even more distressing, they also have an increased risk of Alzheimer's.[267]

Cortisol and adrenalin also affect self-awareness, resulting in people doing and saying things they wouldn't normally do or say. Plus, they heighten self-conscious emotions.

You know what it feels like when you think you're an unwilling centre of attention. It's uncomfortable and you tend to blurt out things and do things that make you even more embarrassed and uncomfortable. A surge of cortisol and adrenalin multiplies this by a large amount. This combination of heightened emotion and high levels of cortisol and adrenalin also has a negative effect on your immune system, which helps to explain why people who are bullied and made to feel demeaned can become physically ill.

Reacting to pressure and stress

Hans Selye said, "It's not stress that kills you, it's how you react to it".

Virtually every job involves pressure and stress at some point, and how you react to it has a significant impact not just on your job success, but also your health and wellbeing. We're an animal species and we tend to react to pressure and threat in one of three basic ways – fight, fight, or submission. Some people go on the attack when threatened, some back away, and some give up.

Unfortunately, all of these behaviours have negative consequences, not just on you but on the people around you.[268] Even if people don't witness your reaction, your feelings are "broadcast" non-verbally and the result is, as we pointed out, that they become contagious.[269]

Putting aside purely accidental or unintentional actions, the effects of what you do are up to you. You don't *have to* react negatively. Thomas Jefferson's advice: "When angry count to ten before you speak", gets to the heart of it. Widen that to when you feel belittled, embarrassed, bullied, afraid, unsettled, or whatever; count to ten and get control of your emotions before you react. We know it's easier said than done, but it's still the right advice.

The problem with pressure and stress is that you tend to allow emotion and self-focus to take over and you either "let it all out", or take actions that are wilful and impetuous. That's a big mistake because while you think your actions will quickly be forgotten or forgiven, *the fact is that their effect on other people is five times greater than the effect of your positive actions.*[270]

People remember negative behaviours and interactions with others more often, in more detail, and with more intensity, than they do positive ones.[271] A node in their brains activates nearby nodes and spreads across their neural network.[272]

Negative reactions to pressure and stress that hinder performance and job success

When you're under pressure or stress do you?

    a) vent your frustration and anger openly,

    b) say you agree with things that you don't agree with

    c) avoid taking any actions that may be contentious.

Defensive-aggressive behaviour

> *"Come back!" the Caterpillar called after her. "I've something important to say." This sounded promising, certainly. Alice turned and came back again. "Keep your temper," said the Caterpillar.*
> Lewis Carroll

If you answered (a), that you "vent your frustration and anger openly when you're under pressure or stressed", that's defensive-aggressive behaviour.

It's the negative, performance hindering behaviour with which people are most familiar and which gets most headlines. It's about dominance and aggression.

It can be a reaction to stress and/or a cause of stress for others. It's the fight response

Sometimes it's very difficult to control the impulse to give vent to anger. Something that has annoyed you triggers stimuli in your hippocampus and amygdala which form emotionally charged memories that linger and fester as you continue to revisit them. As you experience a series of annoying or frustrating incidents over which you have little or no control, the anger builds and then something happens that pushes you over the limit. It can be something small to which you wouldn't normally react, but when your anger has built up without an outlet, it seeks the first possible one in order to release the cognitive pressure. It's called *displacement*, but no matter what it's called, someone, or something, gets some undeserved treatment.

Adam Grant says "venting doesn't extinguish the flame of anger; it feeds it. When we vent our anger, we put a lead foot on the gas pedal of the go system, attacking the target who enraged us." [273] Research done by Brad Bushman shows that venting anger makes you angrier and more aggressive.[274] Think about Bruce Banner, a.k.a. *The Incredible Hulk*, who warns, "Don't make me angry. You wouldn't like me when I'm angry".

So should you suppress your anger? There's a price to pay for suppressing anger. Some interesting research indicates that you experience physical pain more intensely after you have suppressed your anger.[275]

So, a better approach than "putting a lid on it" is to do these four things (we're not saying they're easy, but they help you channel your anger):

1. **Acknowledge that you're angry**. We know that sounds a bit stupid – of course you're angry! But like the process in Alcoholics Anonymous, the first step to changing is acknowledging the problem

2. **Ask yourself why.** What's causing you to be angry? It's important to identify the cause because that allows you to decide what you can do about it and your reaction to it.

3. **Ask yourself the question, "Is it worth getting angry about?"** Is it something you really care about, or is it something trivial? You can get into the habit of becoming annoyed, and the more you do so, the more things become annoying to you.

4. **Ask yourself, "Can I do something about it or is it out of my control?"** Think about this because it's one of the best pieces of advice you can get: *It isn't worth getting angry about things you can't control.*

When the outcome of something has a bearing on your reputation, standing, authority, credibility or power base, it's easy to fall into the trap of defensive-aggressive behaviour. Look behind the behaviour and you'll often find a fear of failure, or a perceived threat to your self-concept.

When you're pressured and stressed, you don't have to vent your anger at people, to lash out and demean them, or to threaten and belittle them. When you do these things it's not to benefit others, it's purely to give yourself the illusion of being strong. As the American philosopher, Eric Hoffer, observed, "Rudeness is the weak man's imitation of strength".

Bullying

We need to be absolutely clear about one thing: bullying is a behaviour, and you can choose how you act. Nobody is compelled to bully others. It's not dictated by their genes and it's not stamped into their DNA. "I can't help it, it's just my personality and I can't change that" is a pitiful (and BS) excuse, and anyone who uses it needs to grow up.

Christine Porath has been researching this behaviour for 20 years. She rather diplomatically calls it, "uncivil behaviour". She says that of the thousands of people at work that she has surveyed, she's found that 98% have experienced defensive-aggressive behaviour and 99% have witnessed it. And she adds, "for every eight people who report working in an uncivil environment, approximately one leaves as a result".[276]

People who have been targets of this type of behaviour reduce their work effort and reduce their commitment to the job.[277]

But the consequences can be much more serious. One research study that surveyed over 4,000 doctors, nurses, and hospital workers found that abusive, insulting, and condescending behaviours were connected to medical errors, and patient deaths.[278] Another study, this time of 4,500 doctors and nurses confirmed this finding. It showed that 71% of respondents linked insulting, condescending and rude behaviour to medical errors they had observed, and 27% "tied the behaviour to fatalities.[279]

Unfortunately, incidents of this type of behaviour don't just have an isolated effect, they're contagious. A study done in 2016 showed that the more rudeness people endured during the day, the less they were able to maintain self-control, and the more they were likely to act rudely to others.[280] Michael Houseman and Dylan Minor researched toxic behaviour and found what they call a *toxic density*. They observed that if you place a toxic worker within 25 feet of another worker, the probability of that person becoming toxic more than doubles.[281]

Stanford professor Bob Sutton has two tests of whether someone is a bully:[282]

1. Does the person who indulges in this behaviour "aim his or her venom at people who are less powerful rather than at people who are more powerful"?

2. Do the targets of the bully's behaviour feel oppressed, humiliated, de-energised, or belittled? And specifically, do they feel worse about themselves?

The negative effect of bullying behaviour by a boss (someone more powerful than you) is much stronger than when it comes from a co-worker, or someone less powerful than you.[283] Whether you like it or not, we have all learned from infancy to be responsive to authority. When someone is seen as powerful, that person's views of us have a stronger effect on how we see ourselves.

People act like bullies for various reasons: envy or resentment of others, seeing others as a threat of some kind, as a means of drawing attention to themselves, or as an attempt to cover up their own failings.

So how should you deal with toxic people and bullies?

➤ At the start of the book we suggested that you **get a soft rubber ball and squeeze it in your right hand** for a few minutes because that would make you feel more positive and get you motivated and eager to achieve things. But it also does something very important, *it makes you recover more quickly from bullying and toxic behaviour.*[284]

➤ One of the ways of dealing with this type of behaviour is **not to react**. It isn't necessarily easy, and taking this approach may not always work, but it's better than becoming obsessed by revenge because that can take you into a deep hole that's hard to get out of.[285] Avoid the temptation to get even.

➤ Perhaps a better way is to **reframe the behaviour**.[286] Can you view the behaviour as a challenge? [287] Can you rise above it? Can you reframe your view of it differently? Can you see it not as something wrong about you but a reflection of the person's own defensiveness and inadequacy? Can you try to see how ridiculous and demeaning it makes the bully look? Is there a funny side that you can privately laugh at when the bully looks ludicrous?

➤ Bullies are often resentful of you and want to bring you down to their level. Bear that in mind because what it's saying to you is that you're better than them.

- Focus on what you do well, what you're good at, and focus on getting better. Psychologists call that attitude *thriving*, and thrivers ride the blows of negative behaviour 35% better than others.[288]

- We've made the point before, but you need energy and vitality to handle the stresses and strains of jobs, and that means you need to take exercise. If you exercise only as little as four hours a week, you're 50% less likely to suffer from burnout.[289]

- Can you try to focus on the good side of bullies? (OK, we know that sounds ridiculous, but relatively few people are all bad.) What actions and sentiments does the bully demonstrate that actually have some merit? Research indicates that if you can focus on a person's good behaviour, and either overlook or forgive some of the bad behaviour, you will reduce the stress.[290]

- Some advice that you'll also hear from time to time is along the lines of "It won't last forever/ things will change/ the person will move to another job", etc.

Think back to our advice about highly toxic workplaces, highly toxic jobs, and highly toxic bosses: *don't engage in fanciful thinking that either it will all go away or that you can handle it without any negative consequences.* Look for the exit and get out as soon as you can.

Conflict avoidance

If you answered (b), that "when you're under pressure or stressed you say you agree with things that you don't agree with", that's conflict avoidance behaviour.

The underlying objective of conflict avoidance is to avoid getting people upset at you, or challenging you, or getting you involved in an argument. So what's wrong with that, you ask? It doesn't hurt anyone does it?

Well, for starters it hurts the organization you work for and has a direct cost. A survey of 656 employees found that by engaging in conflict avoidance they each wasted on average the equivalent of an eight-hour working day and cost about $1500.[291]

But it also affects other people because, as Dr Glenn Marron says, "If you're a conflict avoider, then, by definition, you're a conflict creator ... think of it as setting a fire and then running, leaving it to others to clean up".[292]
Because conflict avoiders sometimes genuinely agree with things but at other times just pretend to agree, the people they work with feel that they don't know where the conflict avoider stands on issues, and they don't know whether it's a real decision or a real opinion. That creates uncertainty, unpredictability, anxiety and stress for them, and you know where that leads.

In spite of what you may think, dodging conflict doesn't actually reduce stress for you. When you say you agree with something with which you don't agree, it takes a toll on you.

Research shows that people who adopt avoidance as a way of dealing with conflict experience higher levels of stress, poor general health, higher exhaustion, and have a higher number of sickness days than those who resolve the conflict through discussion.[293]

Responsibility avoidance

If you answered (c), that "when you're under pressure or stressed you avoid taking any actions that may be contentious", that's responsibility avoidance. In crude terms, it's running away. It's a reaction to stress, threat, uncertainty and frustration that you think will remove you from the cause. The problem with avoiding responsibility is that while it takes the heat off you, it puts the heat on someone else, and that someone else is a person or persons you have to work with.

Putting the heat on someone, and creating grudges as a result, is not a formula for job success. The US president Harry Truman is famous for having a sign on his desk saying, "The Buck Stops Here". There are times when the buck should stop with you; if you don't confront the problem it becomes someone else's problem and that's not likely to make them feel happy about you.

A great deal of responsibility avoidance results from the frustration of being robbed of self-worth, and that's what bad bosses do. There is a high correlation between superiors who engage in defensive-aggressive behaviour – bullying, pressuring, criticizing – and subordinates who become skilled at getting out of the way.[294]

People who are bullied, belittled, and given no recognition for doing things right, but are reprimanded for mistakes, learn to avoid taking any responsibility if possible. But once again there's a cost to you. You may suppress your anger and get out of the way, but it bruises your self-esteem and can affect your health.[295]

One of the causes of responsibility avoidance is work overload. You're doing a job and get asked to take on some additional piece of work - and then another and another and another. The problem is real, and the solution is simple, yet some people find it difficult to implement. It involves knowing when to say "No". Responsibility overload is often related to not being clear about priorities.

People are reluctant to say "No" because they want to be seen as team players, they want to be liked, to feel wanted, to be included, to feel valued. But if you say "Yes" to too many things you're probably saying yes to a lot of unimportant ones. Job success is about focusing on, and doing, the things that produce the most significant results, and not wasting time on things that don't.

What Successful People Do

Andreina Poveda
Marketing Manager, Netflix

Netflix CEO Reed Hastings says "Companies rarely die from moving too fast, and they frequently die from moving too slowly". Netflix is a fast-moving, innovative, constantly developing place to work, and pressure and stress are part of life there. So it's important to know how to deal with it effectively.

Andreina suggests to other people that they acknowledge the feeling of stress as soon as it kicks in. "It's no use pretending that you're not stressed, because until you acknowledge it you will just be rocked by various emotions.
Once you do that you can move on to analysing what's causing the stress". Netflix's organizational culture encourages individuals to listen actively, and seek to understand before reacting or making a decision, and Andreina says this has helped her to handle pressure and stress more effectively.

She says, "Fast moving companies I have worked for continuously change and although this brings a lot of excitement, it also brings new challenges which can create stressful situations. If you're not careful, and you don't keep control of your emotions, you can be tempted to 'let it all out' and vent your stress easily.

But by just taking the step of identifying the root cause of stress, you're able to ask yourself this essential question: Is this something that's really important and not something that's just annoying and not worth getting deeply involved with?"

She makes it clear that doing that isn't about avoiding conflict or avoiding engaging the situation, it's about assessing the issue and being able to decide how much time or energy to spend on it.

Andreina says the massive payoff of doing that means she can look at what's causing the problem and turn it into a challenge. When she does that it gives her a real energy pump, and she is able to turn stress into a strong positive force. That's the time, she says, when you take the challenge head on and you say out loud a few times, "I am excited" and get rid of the stress.

Key points from this chapter

Toxic work places and Toxic work

- ➤ Toxic workplaces and toxic work result in an increased probability of

    - ➤ cancer

    - ➤ heart attack

    - ➤ stroke

    - ➤ deteriorating mental health

    - ➤ suicide

- ➤ They cause headaches, muscle aches, upset stomach, insomnia, loss of sexual desire and/or ability, and frequent colds or infections.

- ➤ They are as bad for women's health as smoking and obesity.

- ➤ Toxic workplaces are the 5th leading cause of death in the USA – 120,000 excess deaths per year.

- ➤ **If you're currently working in a really toxic environment, our urgent advice is *"Get out!"* The** longer you remain in an abusive, toxic environment, the more you will suffer long-lasting emotional damage

➤ *If you are leaving a job, always try to leave on good terms. Never bad mouth your employer.*

Four major stressors that you care about and that you're likely to experience over your work life are:

1. Lack of control

➤ the lower a person's job level, the higher the probability of them experiencing heart disease or death

➤ the lower the level of control people have in their jobs, the higher their level of depression and anxiety

2. Unpredictability

➤ Is what is uncertain and unpredictable important or are you just making it into an issue?

➤ It's easy to get wound up about something that's really not important. A lot of stress is self-generated.

3. Rejection

➤ People have a need to be part of something, to "belong", and to have the support of others.

➤ There is a strong correlation between social support and better health

- Social support relieves stress, regulates insulin, strengthens the immune system, and triggers the release of stress-reducing hormones

- Social support also correlates positively with lower rates of cancer

- One of the most destructive and damaging things is the "like" button on social media because its positive effects are only short-lived.

    - Only 12.5% of people are able to keep the happy feeling from "likes" for as long as an hour

    - Negative social comparisons – *lack* of likes, or comments that mock you, belittle you, threaten you, and strip you of self-esteem, have a much longer lasting effect and lead to depression and anxiety

4. Threats to your self-esteem

- When your self-concept is threatened, and you are also in situations where you have little or no control over things, the situation is hugely stressful

- Remember to ask yourself the question, "How much do I *really* care about this? Is this going to have a major effect on my life, or is it something that I would have just liked to happen (or not happen) that really doesn't make a lot of difference?"

The physical and emotional effects of stress

> ➤ People who continue to suffer from severe stress have poorer memory.

> ➤ High stress levels cause people's emotions to become confused.

> ➤ Prolonged high levels of stress can cause hypertension and heart disease, damage to the immune system, diabetes, depression, and even things like colds and flu.

> ➤ And even more distressing, they also have an increased risk of Alzheimer's.

Reacting to pressure and stress

> ➤ The problem with pressure and stress is that you tend to allow emotion and self-focus to take over.

> ➤ While you think your actions will quickly be forgotten or forgiven, *the fact is that their effect on other people is five times greater than the effect of your positive actions.*

Defensive-aggressive behaviour - Venting your frustration and anger openly when you're under pressure or stressed

> ➤ venting doesn't extinguish the flame of anger; it feeds it.

> ➤ When you feel anger and frustration, do these four things:

>> 1. Acknowledge that you're angry.

>> 2. Ask yourself why.

>> 3. Ask yourself the question, "Is it worth getting angry about?".

>> 4. Ask yourself, "Can I do something about it or is it out of my control?"

Some ideas of how to deal with toxic people and bullies

> ➤ get a soft rubber ball and squeeze it in your right hand for a few minutes

> ➤ Try not to react

> ➤ Try to reframe the behaviour.

> ➤ Focus on what you do well, what you're good at, and focus on getting better.

> ➤ take exercise

> ➤ try to focus on the good side of bullies

➤ Look for the exit and get out as soon as you can

Conflict avoidance - When you say you agree with something with which you don't agree

➤ Dodging conflict doesn't actually reduce stress for you, it increases it

➤ People who adopt avoidance as a way of dealing with conflict experience higher levels of stress, poor general health, higher exhaustion, and have a higher number of sickness days than those who resolve the conflict through discussion

Responsibility avoidance – When you avoid taking any actions that may be contentious

➤ One of the causes of responsibility avoidance is work overload.

➤ Know when to say "No". if you say "Yes" to too many things you're probably saying yes to a lot of unimportant ones.

Chapter 7

What motivates you?

When work is a pleasure, life is joy.
When work is duty, life is slavery
Maxim Gorky

Motivation is a bit like personality. It's about preference, the sorts of things that you prefer doing, that you enjoy most, that make you most comfortable and that give you most satisfaction. The Oxford Dictionary defines it as "a reason or reasons for acting in a particular way". It's a drive that makes you want to do something because the results achieved by doing it are satisfying.

We've specifically stayed away from using the words rewarding or reward in the opening paragraph because of their connotation of money or gifts. We'll discuss money as a motivator later in the chapter. For now, let's just stick with the general idea of satisfaction.

Motivation and job success

What does your motivation have to do with job success? As we pointed out earlier, high-level performance occurs when people do the things that their job requires – when they match their actions to the requirements of the job.

But there is another element to this match-up. It makes a big difference if the job involves doing things that motivate you. If you're motivated by doing something it becomes less like "work" and you give it your best effort. But if you don't enjoy doing something (you're not motivated by it), you find it more difficult to give it 100% for any length of time.

It's important to understand what motivates you and what doesn't. Surprisingly, a lot of people don't know, or haven't thought about it. When they've not been successful at something you hear them make comments like "I never really liked that job". Well, if they never liked it, perhaps they should have been thinking about making a move. Or they should at least have looked for those parts of the job that pushed some of their buttons so they could focus on them as much as possible.

The three most powerful motivators

Recognition

Different things motivate different people, but there are three powerful things that motivate everyone, you included. [296] One of these is recognition.

Recognition takes various forms – for instance, personal recognition, recognition of results, recognition of work practice, recognition of job dedication, recognition of suggestions, etc. – but they all have a positive effect on performance. [297] If you get recognized for what you do at work you're more likely to continue to do it and try to do it better. [298] [299]

When you're given positive recognition for the work you do, you will tend to work harder to achieve good results.[300] You can get a good idea about whether someone gets recognition in their job simply by asking them about what they do. If they talk about their job with some pride and enthusiasm, you know they get recognized for their work.

When you're recognized for doing something, it makes you feel good about yourself and makes you believe that your performance has been rewarded.[301] You don't have to receive any physical reward, just the positive recognition of your actions is enough.

An experiment in a restaurant showed that when the cooks could see the customers enjoying their food, satisfaction with the food increased by 10%. When the diners and the cooks could both see one another, satisfaction increased by 17.3% and service was 13% faster. [302]

If you feel that what you do makes a difference it gives your life more meaning, which in turn makes you feel happier.[303]

It's no accident that when people list companies they like to work for, the ones whose products or services make a positive difference to people's lives tend to feature strongly.

Recognition, and the associated feeling of reward, triggers the release of our old friend dopamine from several sites in the brain.[304] One of the interesting things about recognition is that the effects of the dopamine are significantly stronger when the recognition is unexpected – when you get surprised by getting unpredictably praised publicly for something. If you expect to be recognized for something, and are, it's highly motivating, but when you don't expect it, it's even more so.

If you don't get any recognition for your efforts and achievements at work, please do whatever you can to find another job. Everyone needs to be recognized for who and what they are, or what they do. Nobody needs to be totally ignored and completely forgotten. Life is far too short to put up with that.

Approval

The number one motivator is *approval* – how you are seen by others. Are you admired? Are you respected? Are you valued? Are you liked? Recognition is great, but when it's combined with approval it's even more powerful because everyone wants and needs approval of one kind or another, and everyone will make an effort to achieve it.

Recognition and approval are a very powerful central human need – they're about a sense of belonging, of being a part of something, of being included. Proof that this is such a strong element in our makeup is demonstrated by neurological research that shows that the areas of the brain which light up when the reverse occurs, and a person feels ostracised, are the same as those that are activated by physical pain.[305]

Approval bolsters your self-concept. If you have a job, that means that someone believes you have something to contribute and that you have some value. Jobs provide a feeling of self-worth. Losing your job has the opposite effect.

You might rationalise it as due to something out of your control, such as a company downsizing or a takeover, but when you lose your job you also lose some of your sense of self-worth.

The results of a research study conducted across 75 countries showed the devastating effect of unemployment: it is estimated that the 2008-10 economic crisis was associated with more than 260,000 excess cancer-related deaths.[306]

What makes approval such a powerful motivator is the actual physical process that it triggers. The interesting thing is that while doing something well, or achieving something, increases the dopamine level, getting approval for it by a knowledgeable other (i.e. someone whose opinion is valued) *hugely* increases the surge of dopamine.

Approval also correlates to health and living longer. While wealth plays a role in terms of health because it translates into things like healthier eating, higher levels of sanitation, better access to health care, etc., research indicates a positive correlation between approval from others and health and longevity.[307]

A fascinating research finding about the link between approval and longevity is that Oscar winners live on average four years longer than Oscar nominees.[308] Just being nominated for an Oscar is a huge badge of approval, so it appears that there is no limit to the amount of approval we want. For actors, winning an Oscar is the pinnacle of status. It is the ultimate recognition and approval from knowledgeable others. But once again, showing that you simply can't get enough approval, multiple Oscar winners live an average of *six* years longer than nominees.

The longevity effect even occurs in situations where the subject has been, for a significant period of time, the recipient of worldwide approval from the most discerning and distinguished "knowledgeable others".

Nobel prize winners have all been recognized as being at the top of their fields for a long period of time, but once again, winners live, on average, two years longer than Nobel nominees.[309]

Everyone likes to feel that their efforts and ideas are recognized as being of some significance and worth. If your job provides you with that, you are likely to be successful at it because you will feel motivated. If you're given *approval*, your performance will improve.[310] If your job doesn't provide you with recognition or approval, while you might go through the paces and do it, over time it will have a negative effect on you. We all have a basic human need to explore, experiment and learn and if your job doesn't allow this you should start looking for one that does.[311]

It's useful to remember that people are principally interested in themselves and less interested about others, and to them you're an "other". So don't expect that people will automatically see how great you are and overwhelm you with approval. *The first place to start looking for approval is yourself.* Self-approval is about accepting all of your attributes, positive and negative. You're not perfect, but then nobody is. But first of all, focus on the positives.

Here are two important suggestions:

> ➢ Make a list of the good things about you and what you do, and make sure you look at it at least once a week, or when you're feeling down or have had a bad day.

It's *very important* to remind yourself about your good characteristics and the good things you've done, because it's easy to fall into the trap of focusing on the negatives.

> Take a few minutes at the end of every day to think about what you did, no matter how small, that makes you feel happy about yourself. Congratulate yourself; it's not worth waiting for someone else to do it. There is a real bonus to feeling happy about yourself. It translates not just into mental health but also physical health [312] and longevity. [313]

Autonomy

The third biggest motivational driver is having a feeling of some control over what you do.[314] Control has an element of ownership. If you have some control over something you have a sense of ownership of it, and people value things they own more highly than things they don't own.

In an experiment, individuals were given the choice between receiving a gift of a coffee mug or a large Swiss chocolate bar, and 56% chose the mug while the remaining 44% took the chocolate.

So what's interesting about that? Nothing. But the interesting part came when they were asked if they would trade the mug for the chocolate or vice-versa. Only 10% of the people with the chocolate bar were willing to trade for the mug and only 11% of the mug owners wanted to trade for the chocolate.[315] Once you have some control/ownership over something, you value it more highly and are more committed to it, and you don't want it to fail.

Having some control over your job allows you to do things because you *want* to, not because you *have* to.[316] It doesn't mean you can do whatever you like, when you like. It means that you have some choice. Having autonomy makes you feel more secure. Research shows that people who are able to do things on the basis of their own choice are more productive, are more able to maintain focus, experience less stress and burnout, and generally enjoy higher levels of psychological well-being. [317]

A working conditions survey run by the Dutch research organization TNO showed that low work control is strongly correlated to burnout. Interestingly, they looked at the combined effects of work pressure and autonomy and found that people working under high pressure, but with work control, suffered significantly less burnout than those under pressure with low control over their work. It's not pressure that drives burnout, it's lack of autonomy.

Lack of autonomy is the enemy of commitment and motivation.
A study of 1,000 people who were unemployed as a result of the 2009-2010 recession showed that those of them that moved into jobs with low autonomy and low security suffered even higher levels of stress than people who remained unemployed.[318]

Motivation comes from enabling people to do what they know should be done and what they want to do anyway.[319] If you can find a job where you can do what you enjoy doing, and where doing that makes a positive difference, you will produce your best performance. If you are given tasks where you have a chance to learn, you are more likely to be motivated and engaged than if you're required to do repetitive, rote tasks.

Is money a motivator?

What makes money such a complicated issue is that it represents many things. In a social sense, approval translates into status – how the society in which you live, the culture, the group, the community, the gang, etc., rates and ranks you.[320]

Money is a type of scorecard for success. It's linked to self-esteem as well as esteem from others. It provides freedom of choice. It gives security. Engaging in activities that bring you money delivers a lot of things. But it doesn't necessarily deliver some other things like job satisfaction.

And for some activities, being paid can feel a bit demeaning. To be paid to do something you don't like, don't want to do, or perhaps that you would prefer to do without payment, doesn't give you much of a feeling of self-worth.

A McKinsey survey asked respondents to rate three non-financial motivators – praise from immediate manager (approval), attention from a leader (recognition), and a chance to lead a project or task force (autonomy), versus three highly rated financial incentives – cash bonuses, increased base pay, and stock or stock options. The non-financial incentives were all rated as more effective motivators than the financial incentives. [321]

And that can be taken further: money doesn't compensate for the lack of challenge and learning. In fact it can undermine motivation. Research in 2010 showed that paying people for doing repetitive rote tasks does little to motivate them and, if anything, it undermines their sense of self-determination.[322] You get more pleasure and enjoyment out of things when you take them on purely on your own initiative (autonomy) rather than when they are conditional on payment of some kind. [323]

Looking at 92 studies involving more than 15,000 people, the correlation between pay and job satisfaction turns out to be only 2%.[324] In other words, for 98% of people pay is not the big issue. And it doesn't matter whether people have high pay or low pay or what country they live in.

But don't think that just because 98% of the population say money isn't *the* big issue doesn't mean it's not an important issue. Of course it is! Try living without it.

The basic routes to achieving recognition, approval and autonomy

Research has found that there are three basic ways that people go about achieving recognition, approval and autonomy.[325] David McClelland, who identified them, called them motivational needs, or drives.

Unfortunately, that's a bit confusing, because they aren't the ultimate end result, they're the approach or route to obtain the big three motivators: recognition, approval and autonomy. McClelland labelled them

> ➢ the need for achievement
> ➢ the need for affiliation
> ➢ the need for power

As we said at the start of the chapter, motivation is like personality in that it's about preferences, and these preferences are acquired from experiences in life.[326]

Need for achievement

Need for achievement is about accomplishing things that are a challenge.

The goal of meeting that challenge is to earn recognition and approval not just from others but also from yourself.

For people with this drive, when they complete something difficult or challenging there's a rush of "I did it!" – "I finished the report/ got the sale/ got the job/ completed the marathon/ etc.", and it's accompanied by a dopamine hit.

People who have a high need for achievement display a number of differentiating characteristics:

> They like situations where they are able to take personal responsibility for the outcome and get personal satisfaction when they achieve it

> They tend to be less worried about what others think of them. They know what their goal is, and they know when they achieve it and feel good about it

> They don't like situations where the outcome is a matter of chance; the result has to be due to their own skill and effort

> They set moderately high and challenging goals for themselves – not impossible goals and not goals that are easy to achieve. There has to be a sense of accomplishment

> And they like and require consistent and concrete feedback on their performance. This is most important for high achievers. They need to know how

well or badly they're performing because you can never get better at something unless you know how you're doing

Because of these characteristics, people with a high need for achievement are the most willing to change their behaviour. They will do what is needed to succeed.

Need for Affiliation

Some people seek recognition and approval through affiliation with others. It's the desire to be liked by others, to be part of a group, to enter into warm, personal relationships, and to be in the company of other people.

The achievement drive is all about the individual; the affiliation drive is about being part of a group. High affiliates get recognition and approval from others for being supportive, warm, and likeable, rather than for what they achieve personally. They are less concerned about autonomy although they still need to feel able to make choices about their behaviour.

People who have a high need for affiliation tend to display a number of characteristics:

> They are reluctant to give negative feedback and they find it difficult to behave differently towards poorly performing individuals.

> They find it difficult to check on and manage the behaviour and performance of others

- They tend to shy away from making hard or controversial decisions or from expressing contentious views or opinions.

- They manage on the basis of personal relationships, and their dopamine reward comes from the reciprocal warmth of those relationships.

In terms of change, people with a high need for affiliation are the least willing to change their behaviour. When they do a cost-benefit analysis of changing behaviour vs. improving performance, the perceived cost of losing or destroying relationships often outweighs the perceived benefit of improved performance.

Need for Power

There are two kinds of need for power: p- power and s-power.

P-power is about using power for personal goals. It's self-centred and egotistic. It may get recognition of sorts and it's about having a high degree of autonomy, but whether it attracts approval is another matter.

S-power is about using power to achieve the goals of a group or an organization or society. It's about recognising that you get things done through others. In some sense it's "need for achievement for grown-ups". It attracts recognition and approval as a result of the larger achievement of the group. And, of course, it implies having a fair degree of autonomy.

People who have a high s-power need tend to display a number of characteristics in organizational settings:

- ➤ They are more organization minded and they feel responsible for building and strengthening their organizations

- ➤ They put the interest of the organization ahead of their self-interest

- ➤ They believe in hard work and sacrifice and think that people who show this behaviour should be rewarded for it

- ➤ They like to get things done in an orderly fashion

- ➤ They are less defensive, more willing to seek advice from experts, and have a longer-range view

Finding the best job fit for yourself

One of the things you should explore before accepting a job in a new organization is what their values are and how those values impact the way people work there. If you can find out where employees go for a coffee or a drink after work, go and talk to different people there before you decide on a job.

Stanford professor Bob Sutton says. "When you take a job, take a long look at the people you're going to be working with because the odds are you're going to become like them; they aren't going to become like you. You can't change them. If it doesn't fit who you are, it's not going to work".[327]

Job fit – whether or not your job fulfils your need for achievement, affiliation or power, and whether you get recognition, approval and have some degree of autonomy, is a central factor determining your success. If the fit is good and you enjoy your job, that creates a positive, upward spiral. If you enjoy doing something you tend to do more of it, and the more you do it, the more proficient you become, and the more proficient you are the more successful you're likely to become. The opposite occurs when what you're required to do in your job is not motivating for you – i.e. a bad job fit.

At Google, when an individual's performance is rated in the bottom 5%, the company's solution is to first look at job fit. They have found that when people move to another job which better fits their motivation preferences, their performance typically rises from the bottom 5th percentile to the average, 50th percentile.[328]

What Successful People Do

Jose and Charly Chahin, "The Golden Brothers" Co-Presidents, GRS

In 2008, Jose and Charly Chahin, known as the Golden Brothers, created and developed the GRS brand of home appliances in Central America, and they have expanded the business to various countries around the world.

Jose and Charly are both typical high achievement-driven individuals who continually look for new challenges. When they talk about their business it's clear that they enjoy every moment of it, and they describe what it feels like: "Every day is different and brings new challenges. And every project we move forward successfully fills us with adrenaline".

They are a good example of knowing what motivates you and making sure you don't get into a job that doesn't suit you. They knew that they needed work that offered challenges and they have always been willing to do whatever is necessary to meet those challenges. For instance, because they wanted to do business with China, one of them went to live there for a year to learn about the business culture and to build contacts.

They also understand the power of the three great motivators, recognition, approval and autonomy. They give their people autonomy: "We need effective managers due to our business size" they say, "and as a result, we give them independence and tools so that they get better at what they do".

GRS has a culture of openness to new ideas. Jose and Charly know that their people are a great resource, and they make sure they listen to their ideas and suggestions. They give their people recognition and approval. Employees are able to question processes as well as propose new work formulas. They make the point that "the GRS dream is very aspirational and belongs to more than 165 people. We cannot do it alone. One line of thinking is not enough."

Is it any surprise that with people like Jose and Charly leading it, the company has grown an average of 30% per year?

Key points from this chapter:

➤ If you're motivated by doing something it becomes less like "work", and you give it your best effort. But if you don't enjoy doing something (you're not motivated by it), you find it more difficult to give it 100% for any length of time.

➤ The three most powerful motivators

➤ **Recognition:**

    ➤ Recognition has a strong positive effect on performance. The more that people are given recognition and appreciation, the higher their levels of motivation and performance.

    ➤ When you expect to be recognized for something, and are, it's highly motivating, but when you don't expect it, it's even more so.

➤ **Approval:**

    ➤ *Approval is the number one, most powerful motivator.*

    ➤ Money can be a proxy for status and approval, but approval is the major motivational driver.

> ➢ Approval from others is not only a major motivator, it also leads to better health, wellbeing and longevity.

> ➢ The anticipation of recognition and approval is also a motivator.

➢ **Autonomy**:

> ➢ The third biggest motivational driver is having control over what you do. If you have some control over something you have a sense of ownership of it, and people value things they own more highly.

> ➢ Research shows that people who are able to do things on the basis of their own choice are more productive, are more able to maintain focus, experience less stress and burnout, and generally enjoy higher levels of psychological well-being.

➢ Money doesn't compensate for the lack of challenge and learning, it undermines motivation.

➢ In general, you get more pleasure and enjoyment out of things when you take them on purely on your own initiative (autonomy) rather than when they are conditional on payment of some kind.

- Three major underlying motivational drives that are their route to getting recognition, approval and autonomy are:

    - the need for achievement
    - the need for affiliation
    - the need for power

- The need for achievement

    - is the need to achieve goals and objectives that are challenging, and that earn approval from yourself, but also from others.

- The need for affiliation

    - is the desire to be liked by others, to be part of a group, to enter into warm, personal relationships with others, and to be in the company of others.

- The need for power

    - There are two kinds of need for power: p-power and s-power. P-power is about using power for personal goals. S-power is about using power to achieve the goals of a group.

- Finding a job that you like, that makes you feel good, and that gives you a lot of what you want out of work is something worth thinking about and doing something about.

Chapter 8

Working in teams

Within teams, there is nothing more important than each team member's commitment to a common purpose

John Katzenbach and Douglas Smith

It's relatively rare to find jobs where you work entirely on you own. And even in cases where that is largely the case, you generally have to do some things with other people. Working in teams or with groups of people is part of working life and how you manage it is one of the keys to job success.

Are teams more effective than individuals?

Before we go any further, we need to clear up a popular misconception that teams are always more productive and effective than individuals. They aren't. Harvard professor Richard Hackman says, "I have no question that when you have a team, the possibility exists that it will generate magic, producing something extraordinary – but don't count on it".

He starts off his book, *Leading Teams*, with a short quiz.[329] The first question he asks is, "When people work together to build a house, will the job probably (a) get done faster, (b) take longer to finish, or (c) not get done?

The popular belief is (a) get done faster, but the fact, supported by research, says alternatives (b) and (c) are more likely.

Hackman and his colleagues examined 33 different teams of senior managers and teams of front-line employees in widely diverse occupations and found that only four or five could be classed as operating effectively.[330]

Research consistently shows that a great number of teams perform badly. They encounter problems with coordination, with conflicting objectives, with differing motivations.

Is time spent working cooperatively in teams time well spent?

Over the past ten years the demands for collaborative work have increased by 50%, and knowledge workers spend 85% of their time working with others on email, on the phone, or in meetings.[331] The demands for being a "team player" are persistent and growing but you can do too much of it. It's a route to burnout because, apart from all the collaborative demands, you still have to do your own job.

But there are positive sides to teamwork if you can get it right. Research shows that effective teams develop a collective intelligence that tends to be greater than the average intelligence of the individuals in the group.[332] The key word in that sentence is "effective". Ineffective teams don't produce that result. That's because team effectiveness is not essentially about knowledge, it's about how members communicate and relate to one another.

Communication and interaction in the team have a greater effect on team success than the knowledge of individual team members or the knowledge of the team itself.[333]

What makes teams work well?

How you behave

Behaviour – what you do – drives performance. That is as true for teams as it is for individuals. A major factor in determining performance and results is *how team members act.*

> ➢ If you act positively it will have a positive effect on your teammates, and the team's productivity will increase. If you act negatively that rubs off on your colleagues and team productivity will fall.[334]

> ➢ Having just one persistently negative person in a team will cause its performance to drop by 30% to 40%.[335]

> ➢ Being seen as positive, helpful, and committed helps you achieve job success; being seen as the bad apple that undermines the team's performance does the opposite.

You don't have to be different than your teammates to add to the team. There are various theories and models that claim that high performing teams need to have a balance of people, all with different characteristics – for instance a creative person, a detail-oriented person, a relationships person, etc. However, research shows that's not true.[336]

Information sharing

An important factor in team effectiveness is information sharing. [337] But the *way* information is shared is critical. Researchers studied 699 people in different groups doing different types of tasks that all required cooperation, and what they found to be a key factor in team success was *how individuals in the team treated one another.*[338]

In the high performing teams, the contributions of team members were relatively equal – they each spoke in approximately the same proportion, as opposed to one or two people doing all the talking. The message here is that if you want to be an effective team member, don't try to monopolize the conversation.

Social sensitivity

Just making sure people contribute relatively equally isn't enough in itself, team members need to have social sensitivity – the ability to read the emotional states of their fellow members and to react with empathy.

To work well in a team, you need to try to understand other people and listen to the emotions behind what they say. Are they excited, annoyed, fearful, shy, uncertain, etc.? Social sensitivity can be learned.[339] Being sensitive and aware of other peoples' feeling and emotions pays great dividends.

Research shows that a caring boss is rated more important than pay.[340] Nobody *has* to be insensitive. If you want job success and you need to spend some of your time working in teams, make the effort to try to understand and empathize with your colleagues.

Try to keep these things in mind as you work in a team:

- ➤ You don't have a monopoly on all the good ideas.
- ➤ Your opinions are not always right.
- ➤ Listen to what your team mates have to say and give their ideas and suggestions careful consideration.
- ➤ And if your view is in the minority and you feel that they have all listened to and considered you opinion, it's time to move off your position and go along with them.

Doing those things will make you a good team member.

Having women in the team

As well as relative equality of contributions and social sensitivity, research shows that team effectiveness is positively affected by the proportion of females in the team. [341] The reason for this is that women are generally more socially sensitive than men. While Anita Wooley says, "the more women the better",[342] researchers at Cornell University suggest that "increased interpersonal sensitivity is not necessarily purely the result of females' increased willingness to act with interpersonally sensitive behaviors relative to males.

Rather, it is the result of the increased willingness of individuals – both male and female– to act with these behaviors when interacting with female colleagues".[343] Our experience working with hundreds of teams supports the fact that having a mix of men and women in a team aids effectiveness.

Psychological safety

This is a very important issue. How people treat one another contributes to what social scientists call *psychological safety*, defined as "a shared belief held by members of a team that the team is safe for interpersonal risk taking ... a team climate characterized by interpersonal trust and mutual respect in which people are comfortable being themselves".[344]
It's not about "trigger warnings" or "safe space", it's about being able to feel confident that you can say something, or make a suggestion, and others won't ridicule or embarrass you.

When you're working in a team situation, how comfortable are you about expressing your views openly? Are all the other people in the team comfortable doing that? Can anyone say something, or suggest something, that is "off the wall" without being afraid of being ridiculed? An extensive study by Google found psychological safety to be a central element of effective teams.[345]

Power relationships

One of the things that can act negatively on social sensitivity and psychological safety is power. Research indicates that powerful people often tend to perform badly in teams.[346]

Teams made up of entirely high-power individuals, entirely low-power individuals, and teams with a mix of the two, were given a task involving creativity. The teams were videotaped as they engaged the task and the tapes were rated by independent judges on creativity, conflict, task focus, information sharing, and positive interactions. The teams composed purely of high-powered individuals had fewer positive interactions and shared less information than the low-power or mixed teams.

Unfortunately, organizations are hierarchical and the higher you are the more power you are seen to have. And to get to a high level you have had to be promoted a number of times, and each time you're promoted it makes you think how good you are. After all, you wouldn't have been promoted if you weren't a better performer than others, would you? But it's important not to lose the run of yourself. Ann Landers, the advice columnist, put it delightfully: "Don't accept your dog's admiration as conclusive evidence that you are wonderful".

The most important behaviours of highly effective teams

Do the teams you work in do these things? Research has identified eight behaviours that characterize effective work teams.

1. Creating a shared commitment to what has to be done [347] [348]

2. Making sure people are treated with respect [349]

3. Working for a win-win resolution to conflicts [350] [351]

4. Stating views frankly and openly [352]

5. Holding people accountable for their commitments [353]

6. Giving and accepting open and frank feedback [354]

7. Encouraging contributions from everyone [355]

8. Setting clear priorities and sticking with them [356]

You can, and should, demonstrate all these behaviours, but everyone else in the team also needs to do so if the team is going to operate effectively. The motto of the Three Musketeers sums up what makes a good team: "One for all and all for one".

What Successful People Do

Bruno Mercenari
Co-President, Inova

Bruno joined the international consulting company Accenture after graduating from ITAM and Stanford. The skills and experience he gained there enabled him to join Inova in a leadership position and he is now Co-President of the company.

One of the things he learned at Accenture was the value of hardworking and effective teams.
He says, "We empower people to make decisions and we encourage teams to be positive, to learn how to deal with conflict, and to work together to reach consensus.
That means being committed a common goal, which is a fundamental criterion for effective team performance".

Teams in Inova are held accountable for achieving their agreed objectives. "We have key results that we track them against constantly", he says, "and we encourage people to plan and agree priorities as a team. That helps everyone to focus on the most important things."

Bruno is well aware that a great deal depends on the behaviour of people in a team. One negative person can significantly reduce the effectiveness of the whole team. So he makes a point of dropping in on team meetings from time to time to see how people are operating.

The things he looks for are: Is information shared openly? Does everyone contribute relatively equally? Do people really listen to the points being raised by others or do they appear to just be waiting until someone stops talking so they can make their own point? And he watches to see if team members feel free to put forward ideas and suggestions without the fear of being criticized. Business is changing rapidly, and it is bad policy to shut out new ideas. "Everyone at Inova works hard", he says, "But we are all aligned to the same objectives."

Inova currently has about 1,500 employees, and because it is growing rapidly, the nature of the workforce is changing.

People coming into the organization are from the new generations, millennials and generation Z, and they have different expectations of the workplace – they value transparency, approachability, learning, and a flexible career path. And, as Bruno says, the market is also increasingly made up of these people, so Inova has made sure that its culture is inclusive and open to changing ideas and influences.

Key points from this chapter:

➤ Research consistently shows that a great number of teams perform badly. They encounter problems with coordination, with conflicting objectives, with differing motivations.

➤ Research shows that *effective* teams develop a collective intelligence that tends to be greater than the average intelligence of the individuals in the group, but ineffective ones don't.

➤ Team effectiveness is about how members communicate and relate to one another. Communication and interaction in the team has a greater effect on team success than the knowledge of individual team members.

➤ The major factor in determining performance and results in a team is how team members act. If you act positively it will have a positive effect on your teammates and the team's productivity will increase. If you act negatively that rubs off on your colleagues and team productivity will fall.

➤ Try to keep these things in mind as you work in a team:

> ➤ You don't have a monopoly on all the good ideas.

> ➤ Your opinions are not always right.

- ➤ Listen to what your team mates have to say and give their ideas and suggestions careful consideration.

- ➤ And if your view is in the minority and you feel that they have all listened to and considered you opinion, it's time to move off your position and go along with them.

➤ You don't have to be different than your teammates to add to the team. Research shows that there's no significant relationship between team balance and performance.

➤ In high performing teams, the contributions of team members are relatively equal.

➤ In high performing teams, members have high social sensitivity – the ability to read the emotional states of their fellow members and to react with empathy.

➤ Research shows that team effectiveness is positively affected by the proportion of females in the team.

➤ For a team to operate effectively, there needs to be a sense of psychological safety - a feeling of confidence that you can say something, or make a suggestion, and the team won't ridicule or embarrass you.

➤ Research has identified seven behaviours that characterize effective work teams.

- ➤ Creating a shared commitment to what has to be done

- ➤ Making sure people are treated with respect

- ➤ Working for a win-win resolution to conflicts

- ➤ Stating views frankly and openly

- ➤ Holding people accountable for their commitments

- ➤ Giving and accepting open and frank feedback

- ➤ Encouraging contributions from everyone

- ➤ Setting clear priorities and sticking with them

Advice From An Expert

David Hunt
Head of Panorama Service Delivery, BT
Financial Group

David has had a highly successful career in such diverse areas as strategy, technology, change, and operations. He has built high-performing teams across multiple disciplines and different industries in Australia, Asia and Europe.

This is the advice he would like to share with young people beginning their careers:

Be flexible and curious. The nature of work is changing, and the changes over the coming decades are likely to be truly transformational, as artificial intelligence, automation and other developments cause many jobs that exist today to become defunct
.
New jobs that we may not be able to of conceive today will emerge and take their place.

It's incredibly important to be open to learning new skills, changing roles regularly, working on innovative projects, and above all embracing emerging technologies as they find their way into your workplace.

Put your hand up for (almost) any opportunity that is presented to you. If you fail, fail quickly and learn from the failure. If you succeed, be humble, and make sure everyone who contributed to the success is recognized.

Take ownership of your own destiny. Your success is no one else's responsibility. Find work that makes you happy, challenges you, and gives your life meaning. Give it your all, but don't let it consume you. Make sure you find plenty of time for fun, friends, family, travel, and passions outside of work that energize and fulfil you.

Make an effort to create a genuine personal connection with people with whom you're working on an ongoing basis. Take an interest in their lives. Understand that work is just one part of who they are. Try to find a common interest or experience which can help create an ongoing point of connection. And lastly, be sure to spend as much time listening as speaking, if not more. Listen actively and give your undivided attention.

Visibility is important. Make sure that your actions are both visible and transparent. If you're open with people, they will be open with you. Try to avoid having secret agendas.

David manages his time carefully, making sure he focuses on the top priorities. To avoid being distracted, he recommends setting aside specific times in the day to review and respond to emails, and regularly reviewing your work schedule to ensure that you allocate the majority of your time to what he calls "the big rocks" that you need to deliver to achieve your objectives.

When he's hiring people, he says "While I'm always interested to see the professional experience and academic history of candidates that is relevant for the specific role I am recruiting for, a primary focus is on how the individual will fit with the team and organizational culture. Technical skills required for a role can be taught or developed 'on the job', but these 'softer' factors are much harder to develop".

David says the first quality he looks for in an individual he's thinking of hiring is resilience. "Organizations are increasingly being asked to achieve more with less", he says. "This can create environments that at times are highly pressurized, and individuals' ability to cope with these pressures is a major factor in determining whether they will flourish or fail."

Other qualities he looks for are passion, authenticity, humility, the ability to inspire others, and the courage to speak up and challenge the status quo. "I am also always keen to find candidates who have more to their life than just work, for example being involved in the community, volunteering, studying, or an interest that they pursue with passion".

REFERENCES

[1] Gladwell, M., *Outliers: The story of success*, Penguin Books, 2008.

[2] Schiff, B. B., and Lamon, M., "Inducing emotion by unilateral contraction of the hand muscles", *Cortex*, volume 30, 1994.

[3] Lewandowsky, S., et. al., "Misinformation and its correction: Continued influence and successful debiasing", *Psychological Science in the Public Interest*, volume 13, 2012.

[4] Judge, T. A. and Bono, J. E., "Relationship of core self-evaluations traits – self-esteem, generalized self-efficiency, locus of control, and emotional stability – with job satisfaction and job performance: A meta-analysis", *Journal of Applied Psychology*, volume 86, 2001.

[5] Merzenich, M. M., et. al., "Progression of change following median nerve section in the cortical representation of hand in areas 3b and 1 in adult owl and squirrel monkeys", *Neuroscience*, volume 10, 1983.

[6] Moutsiana, E. A., et. al., "Insecure attachment during infancy predicts greater amygdala volumes in early adulthood", *Journal of Child Psychology and Psychiatry*, volume 56, 2015.

[7] Clark, S. A., et. al., "Receptive fields in the body-surface map in adult cortex defined by temporally correlated inputs", *Nature*, volume 332, 1988.

[8] Werner, K., and Raab, M., "Moving to solution: Effects of movement priming on problem solving", *Experimental Psychology*, volume 60, 2013.

[9] Noice, H., Noice, T., and Kennedy, C., "The contribution of movement and the recall of complex material", *Memory*, volume 8, 2000.

[10] Aberg, M. A., et. al., "Cardiovascular fitness is associated with cognition in young adulthood", *Proceedings of the National Academy of Sciences*, 2009.

[11] Goldstein, A., et. al., "Unilateral muscle contractions enhance creative thinking", *Psychometric Bulletin and Review*, volume 17, 2010.

[12] Palmiero, et. al., "Divergent thinking and age-related changes", *Creativity Research Journal*, volume 26, 2014.

[13] Cotman, C. W., Berchtold, N. C., and Christie, L. A., "Exercise builds brain ealth: Key roles in growth factor cascades and inflammation", *Trends in Cognitive Science*, volume 9, 2007.

[14] Sibley, B. A., and Beilock, S. L., "Exercise and working memory: An individual differences investigation", *Journal of Sport and Exercise Psychology*, volume 29, 2007.

[15] Netz, Y., et. al., "The effect of a single aerobic training session on cognitive flexibility in late middle-aged adults", *International Journal of Sports Medicine*, volume 28, 2006.

[16] Van Praag, H., et. al., "Running increases cell proliferation and neurogenesis in the adult mouse dentate gyrus", *Nature Neuroscience*, volume 2, 1999.

[17] Chapman, S. B., et. al., "Shorter term aerobic exercise improves brain, cognition, and cardiovascular fitness in aging", *Frontiers in Aging Neuroscience*, volume 5, 2013.

[18] Glasper, E. R., and Gould, E., "Sexual experience restores age-related decline in adult neurogenesis and hippocampai function", *Hippocampus*, volume 4, 2013.

[19] Brydon, L., et. al., "Psychological stress activates interleukin-1ß gene expression in human mononuclear cells", *Brain, Behaviour, and Immunity*, volume 19, 2005.

[20] Sotnikov, S. B., et. al., "Bidirectional rescue of extreme genetic predispositions to anxiety: impact of CRH receptor 1 as epigenetic plasticity gene in the amygdala", *Translational Psychiatry*, volume 4, 2014.

[21] Lopez-Maury, L., Marguerat, S., and Bähler, J., "Tuning gene expression to changing environments: from rapid responses to evolutionary adaptation", *Nature Review Genetics*, volume 9, 2008.

[22] Ibid.

[23] Mischel, W., *Personality and Assessment*, Lawrence Earlbaum, 1968.

[24] Nisbett, R., cited in Funder, et. al, "Personality psychology in the workplace: Decade of behaviour", *American Psychological Association*, 2001.

[25] Caspi, A, et. al., "Children's behavioural styles at age three are linked to their adult personality traits at age 26", *Journal of Personality*, volume 71, 2003.

[26] Druckman, D., and Bjork, R. A., (eds.), *In the Mind's Eye: Enhancing Human Performance*, National Academy press, 1991.

[27] Forer, B. R., "The fallacy of personal validation: A classroom demonstration of gullibility", *Journal of Abnormal and Social Psychology*, volume 44, 1949.

[28] Sanitioso, R., Kinda, Z., and Fong, G. T., "Motivated recruitment of autobiographical memories", *Journal of Personality and Social Psychology*, volume 59, 1990.

[29] Fallon, S. J., et. al., "Prefrontal dopamine levels determine the balance between cognitive stability and flexibility", *Cerebral Cortex*, volume 23, 2013.

[30] Hansen, M. T., *Great at Work: How top performers do less, work better and achieve more*, Simon & Schuster, 2018.

[31] Barrick, M. R., and Mount, M. K., "The big five personality dimensions and job performance: A meta-analysis", *Personnel Psychology*, volume 44, 1991.

[32] Schmidt, F. L., and Hunter, J. E., "The validity and utility of selection methods in personnel psychology: Practical and theoretical implications of 85 years of research findings", *Psychological Bulletin*, volume 124, 1998.

[33] Kamran, F., "Does conscientiousness increase quality of life among renal transplant patients?", *International Journal of Research Studies in Psychology*, volume 3, 2013.

[34] "New measure of human brain processing speed", *MIT Technology Review*, August 2009.

[35] Potter, M., et. al., "Detecting meaning in RSVP at 13 ms per picture", *Attention, Perception, and Psychophysics*, 2014.

[36] Ashby, F. G., Turner, B. O., and Horvitz, J. C., "Cortical and basal ganglia contributions to habit learning and automaticity", *Trends in Cognitive Sciences*, volume 14, 2010.

[37] Verplanken, B., and Wood, W, "Interventions to break and create consumer habits", *Journal of Public Policy and Marketing*, volume 25, 2006.

[38] Zanna, M. P., Olson, J. M., and Fazio, R. H., "Self-perception and attitude-behavior consistency", *Personality and Social Psychology Bulletin*, volume 7, 1981.

[39] Corbetta, M., Patel, G., and Shulman, G. L., "The reorienting system of the human brain: From environment to theory of mind", *Neuron*, volume 58, 2008.

[40] Graybiel, A. M., "The basal ganglia and chunking of action repertoires", *Neurology of Learning and Memory*, volume 70, 1998.

[41] Smith, K. S., and Graybiel, A. M., "Habit formation", *Dialogues in Clinical Neuroscience*, volume 18, 2016.

[42] Koole, S., and Spijker, M., "Overcoming the planning fallacy through willpower: Effects of implementation intentions on actual and predicted task-completion times", *European Journal of Social Psychology*, volume 30, 2000.

[43] Bass, B. M., *Bass & Stogdill's handbook of leadership: Theory, research, and managerial applications* (3rd ed.) Free Press, 1990

[44] Burnett, D., *The Idiot Brain*, Guardian Books, 2016.

[45] Critcher, C. R., and Gilovich, T., "Incidental environmental anchors", *Journal of Behavioral Decision Making,* volume 21, 2008.

[46] Martin, S. J., Bassi, S., and Dunbar-Rees, R., "Commitments, norms and custard creams – a social influence approach to reducing did not attends (DNAs)", *Journal of the Royal Society of Medicine,* volume 105, 2012.

[47] Gino, F., Norton. M. I., and Ariely, D., "The counterfeit self: The deceptive costs of faking it", *Psychological Science*, volume 21, 2010.

[48] Aarts, H, and Dijksterhuis, A., "The silence of the library: Environment, situational norm, and social behaviour", *Journal of Personality and Social Psychology*, volume 84, 2003,

[49] Cialdini, R., *Pre-Suasion*, Random House, 2016.

[50] Kuo, F. C., and Sullivan, W. C., "Aggression and violence in the inner city: Effects of environment via mental fatigue", *Environment and Behaviour*, volume 33, 2001.

[51] Darley, J. M., and Batson, C. D., "From Jerusalem to Jericho: A study of situational and dispositional variables in helping

behaviour", *Journal of Personality and Social Psychology*, volume 27, 1973.

[52] Simons, D. J., and Levin, D. T., "Failure to detect changes to people during a real-world interaction", *Psychosomatic Bulletin & Review*, Volume 5, 1998.

[53] Kahneman, D., *Thinking, Fast and Slow*, Farrar, Straus and Giroux, 2011.

[54] Daniels, A. C., *Bringing Out the Best in People*, McGraw-Hill, 2000.

[55] Campbell, W. K., and Sedikes, C., "Self-threat magnifies the self-serving bias: A meta-analytic integration", *Review of General Psychology*, volume 3, 1999.

[56] Kahneman, D, and Klein, G., "Conditions for intuitive expertise, failure to disagree", *American Psychologist*, volume 64, 2009.

[57] Ellis, A. M., et. al., "Newcomer adjustment: Examining the role of managers' perception of newcomer behaviour during organizational socialization", *Journal of Applied Psychology*, volume 102, 2017.

[58] Bassuk, S. S., Church, T. S., and Manson, J. E., "Why exercise works magic", *Scientific American*, August 2013.

[59] Zhang, Z, and Chen, W., "A systematic Review of the relationship between physical activity and happiness", *Journal of Happiness Studies*, 2018.

[60] Chekroud, S. R., et. al., "Association between physical exercise and mental health in 1.2 million individuals in the USA between 2011 and 2015: A cross-sectional study", *The Lancet*, 08 August 2018.

[61] Erickson, K. L., et. al., "Exercise training increases size of hippocampus and improves memory", *Proceedings of the National Academy of Sciences*, volume 108, 2011.

[62] Kircanski, K., Lieberman. M. D., and Craske, M. G., "Feelings into words: contributions of language to exposure therapy", *Psychological Science*, volume 23, 2010.

[63] Sio, U. N., and Ormerod, T. C., "Does incubation enhance problem solving? A meta-analytic review", *Psychological Bulletin*, volume 135, 2009.

[64] Aspinall, P., et. al., "The urban brain: Analyzing outdoor physical activity with mobile EEG", *British Journal of Sports Medicine*, 2013.

[65] Gamble, K. R., et. al., "Not just scenery: viewing nature pictures improves executive attention in older adults", *Experimental Aging Research*, volume 40, 2014.

[65] Kruger, J, and Dunning, D., "Unskilled and unaware of it: How difficulties in recognizing one's own incompetence lead to inflated self-assessments", *Journal of Personality and Social Psychology*, volume 77, 1999.

[66] Baumeister, R. E., et. al., "Ego depletion: Is the active self a limited resource", *Journal of Personality and Social Psychology*, volume 74, 1998.

[67] Gollwitzer, P. M. and Brandstatter, V., "Implementation intentions and effective goal pursuit", *Journal of Personality and Social Psychology*, volume 73, 1997.

[68] Kaplan, S., and Berman, M. G., "Directed attention as a common resource for executive functioning and self-regulation", *Perspectives on Psychological Science*, volume 5, 2010

[69] Steel, P., "The nature of procrastination: A meta-analytic and theoretical review of quintessential self-regulatory failure", *Psychological Bulletin*, volume 133, 2007.

[70] Hofmann, W. R., et. al., "Everyday temptations: An experience sampling study of desire, conflict, and self-control", *Journal of Personality and Social Psychology*, volume 102, 2012.

[71] Newport, C., *Deep Work: Rules for focused success in a distracted world*, Grand Central Publishing 2016.

[72] Ibid.

[73] Aspinall, P., et. al., "The urban brain: Analyzing outdoor physical activity with mobile EEG", *British Journal of Sports Medicine*, volume 49, 2013.

[74] Kachalia, A., et. al., "Liability claims and costs before and after implementation of a medical error disclosure program", *Annals of Internal Medicine*, volume 53, 2010.

[75] Craik, F. L., and Lockhart, R. S., "Levels of processing: A framework for memory research", *Journal of Verbal Learning and Verbal Behaviour*, volume 11, 1972.

[76] Allen, D., *Making it all work: Winning at the game of work and the business of life*, Penguin Books, 2002

[77] Cowan, N., "The magical mystery four: How is working memory capacity limited, and why?", *Current Directions in Psychological Science*, volume 19, 2010.

[78] Cresswell, J. D., Bursley, J. K., and Satpute, A. B., "Neural reactivation links unconscious thought to decision making performance", *Social Cognitive and Affective Neuroscience*, 2013.

[79] Duckworth, A., et. al., "Grit: Perseverance and passion for longer-term goals", *Journal of Personality and Social Psychology*, volume 92, 2007.

[80] Nishida, M., et. al., "REM sleep, prefrontal theta, and the consolidation of human emotional memory", *Cerebral Cortex*, volume 19, 2009.

[81] Tucker, M. A., et. al., "A daytime nap containing solely non-REM sleep enhances declarative but not procedural memory", *Neurobiology of Learning & Memory*, volume 86, 2006.

[82] Gujar, N, et. al., "A role for REM sleep for recalibrating the sensitivity of the human brain to specific emotions", *Cerebral Cortex*, volume 21, 2011.

[83] Naska, A., et. al., "Siesta in healthy adults and coronary mortality in the general population", *JAMA Internal Medicine*, volume 167, 2007.

[84] Strandberg T. E., et. al. "Increased mortality despite successful multifactorial cardiovascular risk reduction in healthy men", *Journal of Nutrition, Health & Aging*, 2018. (accepted)

[85] "The state of the American vacation: How vacation became a casualty of our work culture", *Project: Time Off*, 2017.

[86] Achor, S., and Gielan, M., "The data-driven case for vacation", *Harvard Business Review*, July, 2016.

[87] Hilbrecht, M., and Smale, B., "The contribution of paid vacation time to wellbeing among employed Canadians", *Leisure/Loisir*, volume 40, 2016.

[88] Kivimaki, M. et. al, "Long working hours and risk of coronary heart disease and stroke: a systematic review and meta-analysis

of published and unpublished data for 603,838 individuals", *The Lancet*, volume 386, 2015.

[89] Hansen, M. T., *Great at Work*, Simon &Schuster, 2018.

[90] Shepard, E., and Clifton, T., Are longer hours reducing productivity in manufacturing?", *International Journal of Manpower*, volume 21, 2000.

[91] Virtanen, M., et. al., "Long working hours and cognitive function: The Whitehall II Study", *American Journal of Epidemiology*, volume 169, 2009.

[92] Leproult, R. , et. al., "Sleep loss results in an elevation of cortisol levels the next evening", *Sleep*, volume 10, 1997.

[93] Copinschi, G., "Metabolic and endocrine effects of sleep deprivation", *Essential Pharmacology*, volume 6, 2005.

[94] Krueger, J. M., et. al., "Sleep as a fundamental property of neuronal assemblies", *Nature Reviews Neuroscience*, volume 9, 2008.

[95] Wagner, U., et al., "Sleep inspires insight", *Nature*, volume 427, 2004.

[96] Nagai, M., Hoshide, S., and Kario, K., "Sleep duration as a risk factor for cardiovascular disease – A review of the recent literature, *Current Cardiology Reviews*, volume 6, 2010.

[97] Stickgold, R., "Sleep-dependent memory consolidation", *Nature*, volume 437, 2005.

[98] Hewlett, S. A., and Luce, C. B., "Extreme jobs: The dangerous allure of the 76-Hour workweek", *Harvard Business Review*, December 2006.

[99] Reid, E., "Why some men pretend to work 80-hour weeks", *Harvard Business Review*, April 2015.

[100] Liston, C, McEwen, B. S., and Casey, B. J., "Psychosocial stress reversibly disrupts prefrontal processing and attentional control", *Proceedings of the National Academy of Sciences, USA, 2009*.

[101] Narragon, K., "Subject: Email, we just can't get enough", *Adobe News*, 2015.

[102] Mark, G., et. al., "Email duration, batching, and self-Interruption: Patterns of email use on productivity and stress", *Proceedings of the 2016 CHI Conference on Human Factors in Computing Systems*, 2016.

[103] Vanman, E., Baker, R., and Tobin, S., "The burden of online friends: The effects of giving up Facebook on stress and well-being", *The Journal of Social Psychology*, 20 March 2018.

[104] Levy, S., "To demonstrate the power of Tweets", *Backchannel*, February 2015.

[105] Ibid.

[106] Marulanda-Carter, L., and Jackson, T. W., "Effects of e-mail addiction and interruptions on employees", *Journal of Systems and Information Technology*, volume 14, 2012.

[107] Clark, D., "Actually you should check email first thing in the morning", *Harvard Business Review*, March 7, 2016.

[108] Leroy, S., "Why is it so hard to do my work? The challenge of attention residue when switching between work tasks", *Organization Behavior and Human Decision Process*, volume 109, 2009.

[109] "Frequent multitaskers are bad at it", *The University of Utah News Center*, January 2013.

[110] Gorlick, A., "Media multitaskers pay mental price", *Stanford Report*, August 2009.

[111] Rubinstein, J. S., Meyer, D. E., and Evans, J. E., "Executive control of cognitive processes in task switching", *Journal of Experimental Psychology: Human Perception and Performance*, volume 27, 2001.

[112] Marulanda-Carter, L, and Jackson, T. W., "Effects of email addiction and interruptions on employees", *Journal of Systems and Information Technology*, volume 14, 2012.

[113] Foerde, K., Knowlton, B. J., and Poldrack, R. A., "Modulation of competing memory systems by distraction", *Proceedings of the National Academy of Sciences*, volume 103, 2006.

[114] Dr Glenn Wilson, "The Infomania Study", **www.drglenwilson.com**, 2010.

[115] Vohs, K. D., et. al., "Making choices impairs subsequent self-control: A limited-resource account of decision-making, self-regulation, and active initiative", Journal of Personality and Social Psychology, volume 94, 2008.

[116] Xu, S., and David, P., "Media multitasking and well-being of university students", Computers in Human Behaviour, volume 55, 2016.

[117] Haier, R, J., et. al., "Regional glucose metabolic changes after learning a complex visuospatial/motor task: A positron emission tomographic study" Brain Research, volume 570, 1992.

[118] Dweck, C. S., Mindset: Changing the way you think to fulfil your potential, Random House, 2006.

[119] Pfeffer, J., Power, 2010.

[120] Harmon-Jones, E., and Allen, J. J. B., "The role of affect in the mere exposure effect: evidence from psychophysiological and individual differences approaches", Personality and Social Psychology Bulletin, volume 27, 2001.

[121] Wosinka, W., et. al., "Self-presentational responses to success in the organization: The costs and benefits of modesty", Basic and Applied Social Psychology, volume 18, 1996.

[122] Smith, P. K., et. al., "Lacking power impairs executive functions", Psychological Science, volume 19, 2008.

[123] Robertson, Ian. The Winner Effect, 2012.

[124] Ibid.

[125] Kanter, R. M., Confidence, Random House, 2004.

[126] Schatlo, B., et. al., "Unskilled unawareness and the learning curve in robotic spine surgery", Acta Neurochirurgica, volume 157, 2015.

[127] Regan, D. T., "Effects of a favour and liking on compliance", Journal of Experimental Social Psychology, volume 7, 1971.

[128] Gergen, K. J.,, et. al., "Obligation, donor resources, and reactions to aid in three cultures", Journal of Personality and Social Psychology, volume 31, 1975.

[129] Flynn, F. J., "How much should I give and how often? The effects of generosity and frequency of favour exchange on social status and productivity", Academy of Management Journal, volume 46, 2003.

[130] Cantrill, J. G., and Seibold, D. R., "The Perceptual Contrast Explanation of Sequential Request Strategy Effectiveness", *Human Communication Research*, volume 13, 1986.

[131] Cialdini, R. B., et.al, "Reciprocal concessions procedure for inducing compliance: The door-in-the-face technique", *Journal of Personality and Social Psychology*, volume 31, 1975.

[132] Basuroy, S., Chatterjee, S., and Ravid, A., "How Critical are Critical Reviews? The Box Office Effects of Film Critics, Star power, and Budgets", *Research Gate*, October 2003.

[133] Forsyth, S. M., "Effect of Applicant's Clothes on Interviewer's Decisions to Hire", *Journal of Applied Social Psychology*, volume 20, 1990

[134] Pratt, M. G., and Rafaeli, A., "Organizational Dress as a Symbol of Multilayered Social Identities", *Academy of Management Journal*, volume 40, 1997.

[135] Bailenson, J. N., et. al., "Facial Similarity Between Voters and Candidates Causes Influence", *Public Opinion Quarterly*, volume 72, 2008.

[136] Burger, J. M., et. al., "What a coincidence! The effects of incidental similarity on compliance", *Personality and Social Psychology Bulletin*, volume 30, 2004.

[137] Know, R. E., and Inkster, A. J., "Post Decisional Dissonance Reduction", *Journal of Personality and Social Psychology*, volume 8, 1968.

[138] Baca-Motes, K., et. al., "Commitment and behavior change: Evidence from the field", *Journal; of Consumer Research*, volume 39, 2013.

[139] Drachman, D., deCarufel, A., and Insko, A. C., "The extra credit effect in interpersonal attraction", *Journal of Experimental Social Psychology*, volume 14, 1978.

[140] Westphal, J. D., and Stern, I., "The other pathway to the boardroom: Interpersonal influence behaviour as a substitute for elite credentials and majority status in obtaining board appointments", *Administrative Science Quarterly* ,volume 51, 2006.

[141] Cavazza, N., "The tone dilemma: Comparing the effects of flattery and verbal aggression in a political speech", *Journal of Language and Social Psychology*, volume 35, 2017.

[142] Sezer, O., Brooks, A., and Norton, M. I., "Backhanded compliments: How negative comparisons undermine flattery", *Harvard Business School, Working Paper 18-082*, 2018.

[143] Koforda, K., and Tschoeglb, A. E., "The market value of rarity", *Journal of Economic Behavior and Organization*, volume 34, 1998.

[144] Worchel, et. al., "Effects of Supply and Demand on Ratings of Object Value", *Journal of Personality and Social Psychology*, volume 32, 1975.

[145] Cialdini, R. B., *Pre-suasion*, 2016.

[146] Flynn, F. J., and Lake, V. B. B., "If Your Need Help Just Ask: Underestimating Compliance with Direct Questions for Help", *Journal of Personality and Social Psychology*, volume 95, 2008.

[147] Nadler,A., Ellis, S., and Bar, I., "To Seek or Not to Seek: The relationship Between Help Seeking and Job Performance Evaluations as Moderated by Task-Relevant Expertise", *Journal of Applied Social Psychology*, volume 33, 2003.

[148] Freedman, J. L., and Fraser, S.C., "Compliance Without Pressure: The Foot-in-the-Door Technique", *Journal of Personality and Social Psychology*, volume 4, 1966.

[149] Bartlett, M. Y., et. al., "Gratitude: prompting behaviours that build relationships", *Cognition and Emotion*, volume 26, 2011.

[150] Argyle, M., et. al., "The communication of inferior and superior attitudes by verbal and nonverbal signals", *British Journal of Clinical Psychology*, volume 9, 1970.

[151] Aguinas, H., Simonsen, M. M., and Pierce, C. A., "Effects of nonverbal behaviour on perceptions of power bases", *Journal of Social Psychology*, volume 138, 1998.

[152] Burgoon, J. K., Birk, T. Pfau, M,. "Nonverbal behaviours, persuasion, and credibility", *Human Communication Research*, volume 17, 1990.

[153] Costerhof, N. N., and Todorov, A., "Shared perceptual basis of emotional expressions and trustworthy impressions from faces", *Emotion*, volume 9, 2009.

[154] Willis, J. and Todorov, A., "First impressions: Making up your mind after a 100-ms exposure to a face", *Psychological Science*, volume 17, 2006.

[155] Ambady, N., and Rosenthal, R., "Thin slices of expressive behaviour as predictors of interpersonal consequences: A meta-analysis", *Psychological Bulletin*, volume 111, 1992.

[156] Cuddy, A. J. C., Kohut, M. and Neffinger J., "Connect, then lead: To exert influence you must balance competence with warmth", *Harvard Business Review*, July-August 2013.

[157] Todorov, A, Pakrashi, M. and Oosterhof, N. N., "Evaluating faces on trustworthiness after minimal time exposure" *Social Cognition*, volume 27, 2009.

[158] Grandey, A. A., et. al., "Is service with a smile enough? Authenticity of positive displays during service encounters", *Organizational Behaviour and Human Decision Processes*, Volume 96, 2005.

[159] Aviezer, H., et. al., "Body cues, not facial expressions, discriminate between Intense positive and negative emotions", *Science*, volume 388, 2012.

[160] Klofstad, C. A., Anderson, R. C., and Peters, S., "Sounds like a winner: voice pitch influences perception of leadership capacity in both men and women", *Proceedings of The Royal Society of Biological Sciences*, volume 279, 2012.

[161] Centorrino, S., et. al., "Honest signalling in trust interactions: Smiles rated as genuine induce trust and signal higher earning opportunities", *Evolution and Human Behaviour*, volume 36, 2015.

[162] Beilock, S., *How the Body Knows its Mind*, Atria Books, 2015.

[163] Chen, F. S., et. al,, "Tell me more: The effects of expressed interest on receptiveness during dialog", *Journal of Experimental Social Psychology*, volume 46, 2010.

[164] Goldman, A. I., and Sripada, C. S., "Simulationist models of face-based emotion recognition", *Cognition*, volume 94, 2005.

[165] Winerman, L., "The mind's mirror", *American Psychological Association*, volume 36, 2005.

[166] Davis, M., "The role of the amygdala in fear and anxiety", *Annual Review of Neuroscience*, volume 15, 1992.

[167] van Swol, L. M., "The effects of nonverbal mirroring on perceived persuasiveness, agreement with an imitator, and reciprocity in a group discussion", *Communication Research,* August 2003.

[168] Neal, D. T., and Chartrand, T. L., "Embodied emotion perception amplifying and dampening facial feedback modulates emotion perception accuracy", *Social Psychological and Personality Science,* volume 2, 2011.

[169] Goffman, E., *The Presentation of Self in Everyday Life,* Random House, 1956.

[170] Schienker, B. R., Dlugolecki, D. W., and Doherty, K., "The impact of self-presentations on self-appraisals and behavior: The power of public commitment", *Personality and Social Psychology Bulletin,* volume 20, 1994.

[171] Carney, D. R., Cuddy, A. J., and Yap, A. J., "Power posing: Brief nonverbal displays affect neuroendocrine levels and risk tolerance", *Psychological Science,* volume 10, 2010.

[172] Schubert, T. W., and Koole, S. L., "The embodied self: Making a fist enhances men's power-related self-conceptions", *Journal of Experimental Social Psychology,* volume 45, 2009.

[173] Brinol, P., Petty, R. E., and Wagner, B., "Body posture effects on self-evaluation: A self-validation approach", *European Journal; of Social Psychology,* volume 39, 2009.

[174] Skipper, J. I., et. al., "Speech-associated gestures, Broca's area, and the human mirror system", *Brain and Language,* volume 101, 2007.

[175] Niedenthal, P. M., "Embodying emotion", *Science,* volume 316, 2007.

[176] Ibid.

[177] Dimburg, U., and Söderkvist, S., The voluntary facial action technique: A method to test the facial feedback hypothesis", *Journal of Nonverbal Behaviour,* volume 35, 2011.

[178] Wild, B., et. al., "Why are smiles contagious? An fMRI study of the interaction between perception of facial affect and facial movements", *Psychiatry Research,* volume 123, 2003.

[179] Gutman, R., "The Untapped Power of Smiling", *Forbes*, March 22, 2011.

[180] Abel, E. L., and Kruger M. L., "Smile intensity in photographs predicts longevity", *Psychological Science*, volume 21, 2010.

[181] Kraft, T. L., "Grin and bear It: The influence of manipulated facial expression on the stress response", *Psychological Science*, volume 23, 2012.

[182] Wilkinson, D., et. al., "Feeling socially powerless makes you more prone to bumping into things on the right and induces leftward line bisection error" *Psychonomic Bulletin and Review*, volume 17, 2010.

[183] Roskes, M., et. al., "The right side? Under Time pressure, approach motivation leads to right-oriented bias", *Psychological Science*, volume 22, 2011.

[184] Hatfield, E., et. al., *Emotional Contagion*, Cambridge University Press, 1994.

[185] Bargh, J., *Before You Know It: The unconscious reasons we do what we do*, William Heinemann, 2017.

[186] Williams, L. E., and Bargh, J. A., "Experiencing physical warmth promotes emotional warmth", *Science*, volume 322, 2008.

[187] Kang, Y., et. al., "Physical temperature effects on trust behaviour: the role of insula", *Social Cognitive and Affective Neuroscience*, volume 6, 2011.

[188] Ijzerman, H., et. al., "Cold-blooded loneliness: Social exclusion leads to lower skin temperatures", *Acta Psychologica*, volume 140, 2012.

[189] Harmon, K., "Hard chairs drive hard bargains: Physical sensations translate to social perceptions", *Scientific American*, June 2010.

[190] North, A. C., Hargreaves, D.J., and McKendrick, J., "In-store music affects product choice", *Nature*, volume 390, 1997.

[191] Howard, D. J., and Gengler, C., "Emotional contagion effects on product attitudes", *Journal of Consumer Research*, volume 28, 2001.

[192] Meisner, B. A., "A meta-analysis of positive and negative age stereotype priming effects on behaviour among older adults",

Journal of Gerontology Series B: Psychological Sciences and Social Sciences, volume 67, 2012.

[193] Ian Robertson, *The Stress Test: How Pressure Can Make You Stronger and Sharper*, Bloomsbury, 2016.

[194] Berens, C., "Report: Anxiety can improve work performance", *Inc.*, June 19, 2012.

[195] Parker, C. B., "Embracing stress is more important than reducing stress", *Stanford News*, May 7, 2015.

[196] Yun, H. J., et. al., "Chronic stress accelerates learning and memory impairments and increases amyloid deposition in APPV717I-CT100 transgenic mice, an Alzheimer's disease model", *The FASEB Journal*, February 8, 2006.

[197] Crum, A. J., Salovey, P, and Achor, S., "Rethinking stress: The role of mindsets in determining the stress response", *Journal of Personality and Social Psychology*, volume 104, 2013.

[198] Boudarene, M., Legros, J. J., and Timsit-Berthier, M., "Study of the stress response: Role of anxiety, cortisol and DHEAs", *L'Encephale*, volume 28, 2001.

[199] Wemm, S., et. el., "The role of DHEA in relation to problem solving and academic performance", *Biological Psychology*, volume 85, 2010.

[200] Ibid.

[201] Morgan, C. A., et. al., "Relationships among plasma dehydroepiandrosterone sulfate and cortisol levels, symptoms of dissociation, and objective performance in humans exposed to acute stress", *Archives of General Psychiatry*, volume 61, 2004.

[202] Seery, M. D., Holman, A., and Silver, R. C., "Whatever does not kill us: Cumulative lifetime adversity, vulnerability and resilience", *Journal of Personality and Social Psychology*, volume 99, 2010.

[203] Allison, A. L., et. al., "Fight, flight, or fall: Autonomic nervous system reactivity during skydiving", *Personality and Individual Differences*, volume 53, 2012.

[204] Von Dauwens, B., et. al., The social dimension of stress reactivity: Acute stress increases prosocial behaviour in humans", *Psychological Science*, volume 23, 2012.

[205] Lederbogen, F., et. al., "City Living and Urban Upbringing Affect Neural Social Stress Processing in Humans", *Nature*, 2011.

[206] Crum, A. J., *Rethinking stress: The role of mindsets in determining the stress response*, PhD Dissertation, Yale, 2012.

[207] Elliot, A. J., et. al., "Cross cultural generality and specificity in self-regulation: Avoidance of personal goals and multiple aspects pf well-being in the United States and Japan", *Emotion*, volume 12, 2012.

[208] Holahan, C. J., et. al., "Stress generation, avoidance coping, and depressive symptoms: A 10-year model", *Journal of Consulting and Clinical Psychology,* volume 73, 2008.

[209] Foulk, T., Woolum, A., and Erez, A., "catching rudeness is like catching a cold": The contagion effect of low-intensity negative behaviours", *Journal of Applied Psychology*, volume 101, 2016.

[210] Waters, S. F., West, T, V., and Mendes, W. B., "Physiological covariation between mothers and infants", *Psychological Science*, January 2014.

[211] Crum, A. J., et. at., "The role of stress mindset in shaping cognitive, emotional and physiological responses to challenging and threatening stress", *Anxiety, Stress and Coping*, 2017.

[212] Crum, A. J., et. al., "Mind over milk-shakes: Mindsets, not just nutrients, determine ghrelin response", *Health Psychology*, volume 30, 2011.

[213] Howe, L. C., Goyer, J. P., and Crum, A. J., "Harnessing the placebo effect: Exploring the influence of physician characteristics on placebo effect", *Health Psychology*, 2017.

[214] Levy, B., et. al., "Age stereotypes held earlier in life predict cardiovascular events in later life", *Psychological Science*, volume 20, 2009.

[215] Levy, B., et. al., "Physical recover after acute myocardial infarction: Positive age self-stereotypes as a resource", *International Journal of Aging and Human Development*, volume 62, 2006.

[216] Ian Robertson, *The Stress Test*, Bloomsbury, 2016.

[217] Brooks, A., "Get Excited: Reappraising Pre-performance Anxiety as Excitement", *Journal of Experimental Psychology General*, volume 143, 2014.

[218] Christine Porath, "Managing Yourself: An Antidote to Incivility", *Harvard Business Review*, April, 2016.

[219] Lutgen-Sandvik, P., "Take this job and …:Quitting and other forms resistance to workplace bullying", *Communication Monographs*, volume 73, 2006.

[220] American Institute of Stress, www.stress.org/workplace-stress/

[221] www.forthwithlife.co.uk , February 4, 2018.

[222] "Perceived Life Stress: 2014", Statistics Canada, www.105.statcan.gc.ca

[223] Bergland, C., "Stress in America is gnawing away at our overall well-being", *Psychology Today*, November 2017.

[224] Work related Stress, Anxiety and Depression Statistics in Great Britain 2016, *Health and Safety Executive, V1*, November 2016.

[225] Goh, J., Pfeffer, G., and Zenios, S. J., "The Relationship Between Workplace Stressors and Mortality and Health Costs in the United States", *Management Science*, Published on line in Articles in Advance, March 13, 2015.

[226] "Prolonged exposure to work-related stress thought to be related to certain cancers", *Science Daily*, January 17, 2017.

[227] Steptoe, A, and Kivimaki, M., "Stress and cardiovascular disease", *Nature Reviews Cardiology*, volume 9, 2012.

[228] Tsutsumi, A., Kayaba, K., and Ishikawa, S., "Impact of occupational stress on stroke across occupational classes and genders", *Social Science and Medicine*, volume 72, 2011.

[229] Ramirez, A. J., et. al, "Mental health of hospital consultants: the effects of stress and satisfaction at work", *The Lancet*, volume 347, 1996.

[230] Schneider, B., et. al. "Impact of employment status and work-related factors on risk of completed suicide", *Psychiatry Research*, volume 190, 2011.

[231] www.webmd.com

[232] Slopen, N., et. al., "Job strain, job insecurity and incident cardiovascular disease in the women's health study: Results from a 10-year prospective study", *PLoS ONE*, volume 7, 2012.
[233] Pfeffer, J., *Dying for a Paycheck*, Harper Business, 2018.
[234] Nelson, D. I., et. al. "The global burden of selected occupational diseases and injury risks: Methodology and summary", *American Journal of Industrial Medicine*, volume 48, 2005.
[235] Mackey, J. D., et. al., "Abusive supervision: A meta-analysis and empirical review", *Journal of Management*, volume 23, 2017.
[236] Hoorens, V., "Self-enhancement and superiority biases in social comparison", *European Review of Social Psychology*, volume 4, 1993.
[237] Axsom, D., "Effort Justification", in *Encyclopedia of Social Psychology*, 2007, Baumeister, R. F. and Vohs, K. D., eds.
[238] McGonigal, K., *The Upside of Stress*, Penguin Random House, 2018.
[239] Marmot, M. G., et. al., "Employee grade and coronary heart disease in British civil servants", *Journal of Epidemiology and Community Health*, volume 32, 1978.
[240] Spell, C. S. and Arnold, T., "An appraisal of justice, structure, and job control as antecedents pf psychological distress", *Journal of Organizational Behaviour*, volume 28, 2007.
[241] Cloutier, J., et. al., "Understanding the Effect of Procedural Justice on Psychological Distress", INTERNATIONAL JOURNAL OF STRESS MANAGEMENT, 2017. (Advance online publication)
[242] Seligman, M. E. P., "Learned helplessness", *Annual Review of Medicine*, volume 23, 1972.
[243] Frankl, V., *Man's search for Meaning*, Ebury Publishing, 2008.
[244] O'Driscoll, M. P., and Beehr, T. A., "Supervisory behaviours, role stressors and uncertainty as predictors of personal outcomes for subordinates", *Journal of Organizational Behaviour*, volume 15, 1994.
[245] Bauneister, R. F., and Leary, M. R., "The need to belong: Desire for inter-personal attachments as a fundamental human motivation", *Psychological Bulletin*, volume 117, 1995.

[246] Broadhead, W. E., et. al., "the epidemiological evidence for a relationship between social support and health", *American Journal of Epidemiology*, volume 117, 1983.

[247] Belanger, et. al., "Sources of support associated with health and quality of life: A cross-sectional study among Canadian and Latin American older adults", *BMJ Open*, volume 6, 2016.

[248] "The health benefits of strong relationships", *Harvard Health Publishing*, Harvard Medical School, December 2010.

[249] Uchino, B. N., "Social support and health: A review of physiological processes potentially underlying risks to disease outcomes", *Journal of Behavioral Medicine*, volume 4, 2006.

[250] Jankowski, M., et. al., "Xxytocin in the heart regeneration", *Recent Advances in Cardiovascular Drug Discovery*, August 2102.

[251] Meyer, M. L., Williams, K. D., and Eisenberger, N. I., "Why social pain can live on: Different neural mechanism are associated with relieving social pain and physical pain", *PLoS One*, volume 10, 2015.

[252] Tait, A., "Both hugely uplifting and depressing: How do social media Likes affect you?", *New Statesman*, January 27, 2017.

[253] Seabrook, E. M., Kern, M. L., and Rickard, N. S., "Social networking sites, depression, and anxiety: A systematic review", *JMIR Mental Health*, volume 3, 2016.

[254] Sally S. Dickerson, "Emotional and Physiological Responses to Social-Evaluative Threat", *Social and Personality Psychology*, 2008.

[255] Lehman, B. J., et. al., "Physiological and emotional responses to subjective social evaluative threat in daily life", *Anxiety, Stress & Coping*, volume 28, 2015.

[256] Dickerson, S. S., and Kemeny, M. E., "Acute Stresses and Cortisol Responses", *Psychological Bulletin,* 2004.

[257] Ibid.

[258] Keller, A., et. al., "Does the Perception that Stress Affects Health Matter? The Association with Health and Mortality", *Health Psychology,* volume 31, 2012.

[259] Lepine, J. A., Podsakoff, N. P., and Lepine, M. A., "A meta-analytic test of the challenge stressor-hindrance stressor framework: An explanation for inconsistent relationships

among stressors and performance", *Academy of Management Journal*, volume 48, 2005.

[260] McGonigal, K., *The Upside of Stress*, Penguin Random House, 2018.

[261] Weitzman, E. D., et. al., "Twenty-four-hour pattern of the episodic secretion of cortisol in normal subjects", *Journal of Clinical Endocrinology and Metabolism*, volume 33, 1971.

[262] Ulrich, R. S., et. al., "Stress recovery during exposure to natural and urban environments". *Journal of Environment Psychology*, volume 11, 1991.

[263] R. M. Sapolsky, "Why Stress is Bad for Your Brain", *Science*, volume 273, 1996.

[264] Chen, L., et. al, "impact of acute stress on human brain microstructure: An MR diffusion study of earthquake survivors", *Human Brain Mapping*, volume 34, 2013.

[265] Erbas, Y., et. al., "Why I don't always know what I'm feeling: The role of stress in within-person fluctuations in emotional differentiation", *Journal of Personality and Social Psychology*, volume 115, 2018.

[266] Cohen, S., Tyrrell, D. A. J., and Smith, A. P.," Psychological Stress and Susceptibility to the Common Cold", *New England Journal of Medicine*, August 1991.

[267] Wilson, R. S., et. al, "proneness to psychological distress is associated with risk of Alzheimer's disease", *Neurology*, volume 61, 2002.

[268] Bear, A, and Rand, D/ G., "Intuition, deliberation and the evolution of cooperation", *Proceedings of the National Academy of Sciences*, November 2015.

[269] Foulk, T., Erez, A., and Woolum, A., "Catching Rudeness is Like Catching a Cold: The Contagion Effects of Low-Intensity Negative Behaviours", *Journal of Applied Psychology*, , volume 101, number 1, 2016

[270] Andrew Miner, Theresa Glomb, and Charles Hulin, "Experience sampling mood and its correlates at work", *Journal of Occupational and Organizational Psychology*. 2005.

[271] M. T. Dasborough, "Cognitive Asymmetry in Employee Emotional Reactions to Leadership Behaviours", *Leadership Quarterly*, volume 17, 2006.

[272] Stanley, M. L. et. al., "Defining Nodes in Complex Brain Networks", *Frontiers in Computational Neuroscience*, Published online, November 22, 2013.

[273] Adam Grant, *Originals: How Non-conformists change the world*, W H Allen, 2016.

[274] Bushman, B. J., "Does venting anger feed or extinguish the flame?", *Personality and Social Psychology Bulletin*, June 2002

[275] Quartana, P. J., and Burns, J. W., "Painful consequences of anger suppressions", *Emotion*, volume 7, 2007.

[276] Christine Porath, "Managing Yourself: An Antidote to Incivility", *Harvard Business Review*, April 2016.

[277] Pearson, C. M., and Porath, C. L., "On incivility, its impact and directions for future research", in *The Dark Side of Organizational Behaviour*, Griffin and O'Leary-Kelly, Wiley, 2004

[278] Christine Porath, and Amir Erez, "How Rudeness takes its toll", *The Psychologist,* July 2011.

[279] Rosenstein. A. H., and O'Daniel, M., "A Survey of the Impact of Disruptive Behaviours and Communication Defects on Patient Safety", *Joint Commission Journal on Quality and Patient Safety*, volume 34, 2008.

[280] Foulk, T, Woolum, a., and Erez, A., "Catching rudeness is like catching a cold: The contagion effects of low-intensity negative behaviors", *Journal of Applied Psychology*, volume 101, 2016.

[281] Houseman, M., and Minor, D., ""Toxic Workers", *Harvard Business School Strategy Unit Working Paper,* No. 16-057, 2015.

[282] Sutton, R., *The No Asshole Rule: Building a civili9sed workplace and surviving one that isn't,* Sphere, 2207.

[283] Hershcovis, M. S., and Barling, J., "Towards a multi-foci approach to workplace aggression: A meta-analytic view of outcomes from different perpetrators", *Journal of Organizational Behaviour*, volume 31, 2010.

[284] Davidson, R. J., and Begley, S., *The Emotional Life of Your Brain: How its Unique Patterns Affect the Way You Think, Feel, and Live – And How You can Change Them*, Hudson Street press, 2012.

[285] Moreno-Jimenez, B., et. al., "The moderating effects of psychological detachment and thoughts of revenge in workplace

bullying", *Personality and Individual Differences*, volume 46, 2009.

[286] Yagil, D, Ben-Zur, H., and Tamir, I., "Do employees cope effectively with abusive supervision at work? An exploratory study", *International Journal of Stress Management*, volume 18, 2011.

[287] Alter, M.A., et. al., "Rising to the threat: Reducing stereotype threat by reframing the threat as a challenge", *Journal of Experimental Social Psychology*, volume 46, 2010.

[288] Porath, C. L., "An antidote to Incivility", *Harvard Business Review*, April 2016.

[289] Toker, S., and Biron, M., "Job burnout and depression: Unravelling their temporal relationship and considering the role of physical activity", *Journal of Applied Psychology*, volume 97, 2012.

[290] Van Oyen Witvliet, C., et. al., Granting forgiveness or harbouring grudges: Implications for emotion physiology and health", *Psychological Science*, volume 12, 2001.

[291] Vitalsmarts Research, www.vitalsmarts.com, March 2010.

[292] Marron, G., "Conflict Avoidance", www.glennmarron.com, May 26, 2014.

[293] Hyde, M., et. al., "Workplace conflict resolution and the health of employees in the Swedish and Finnish units of an industrial company", *Social Science & Medicine*, October 2006.

[294] Corina, L. M., and Magley, V. J., "Patterns and profiles of response to incivility in organizations", *Journal of Occupational Health Psychology*, volume 14, 2009.

[295] Hershcovis, et. al., "Targeted workplace incivility: The roles of belongingness, embarrassment and power", *Journal of Organizational Behaviour*, 2017.

[296] In Reeve, S.G., *et. al*, *Motivation and Emotion*, 1986.

[297] Chikungwa, T., and Shingirayi, F. C., ""An Evaluation of Recognition on Performance as a Motivator: A Case of Eastern Cape Higher Education Institution", *Mediterranean Journal of Social Sciences*, volume 4, 2013.

[298] Brun, J-P, and Dugas, N., "An analysis of employee recognition: Perspectives on human resources practices", *The International Journal of Human Resource Management*, volume 19, 2008.

[299] Baskar, D., and Rajkumar, K. R., "A Study on the Impact of Rewards and Recognition on Employee Motivation", *International Journal of Science and Research*, volume 4, 2015.

[300] Pelham, B. W., Carvallo, M., and Jones, J. T., "Implicit egotism", *Current Directions in Psychological Science*, volume 14, 2005.

[301] Ashby, F. G., Isen, A. M., and Turken, A. U., "A Neuropsychological Theory of Positive Affect and Its Influence on Cognition", *Psychological Bulletin*, volume 106, 1999.

[302] Ryan W. Buell, Tami Kim, and Chia-Jung Tsay, "Creating Reciprocal Value Through Operational Transparency", *Social science Research Network*, November 24, 2015.

[303] Kets de Vries, M., *The Happiness Equation*, Vermillion, 2000.

[304] Izuma, K., Saito, DN., and Sadato, N., "Processing of social and monetary rewards in the human striatum", *Neuron*, volume 58, 2208.

[305] Eisenberger, N. I., "Social Pain and the Brain: Controversies, Questions, and Where to go from Here", *Annual Review of Psychology*, volume 66, 2015.

[306] Maruthappu, M., et. al., "Economic downturns, universal health coverage, and cancer mortality in high-income and middle-income countries, 1990-2010: A longitudinal analysis", *The Lancet*, volume 388, 2016.

[307] Smith, G. D., et. al., "Socioeconomic differentials in mortality: Evidence from Glasgow graveyards", *British Medical Journal*, volume 305, 1992.

[308] Redelmeir, D. A., and Singh, S. M., "Survival in Academy Award-winning actors and actresses", *Annals of Internal Medicine*, volume 134, 2006.

[309] Rablen, M. D., and Oswald, A. J., "Mortality and Immortality; The Nobel Prize as an experiment into the effect of status upon longevity", *Journal of Health Economics*, volume 27, 2008.

[310] Guéguen, N., Martin, A.,, and Andrea, C. R., """I am sure you'll succeed': When a teacher's verbal encouragement of success increases children's academic performance", *Learning and Motivation*, volume 52, 2015.

[311] Cable, D., "Why People Lose Motivation – and What Managers Can Do to Help", *Harvard Business Review,* March 2016.

[312] Ray, M. N., Saag, K. G., and Allison, J. J., "Health and happiness among older adults: A community-based study", *Journal of Health Psychology*, Volume 13, 2009.

[313] Smith, G. D., et. al., "Socioeconomic differentials in mortality: Evidence from Glasgow graveyards", *British Medical Journal*, 1992.

[314] Ryan, R. M. and Deci, E. L., "Self-determination theory and the facilitation of intrinsic motivation, social development, and well-being", *American Psychologist*, volume 55, 2000.

[315] Knetsch, J. L.," The endowment effect and evidence of nonreversible indifference curves", *American Economic Review*, volume 79, 1989.

[316] Deci, E. L., and Ryan, R. M., "Facilitating Optimal Motivation and Psychological Well-Being Across Life's Domains", *Canadian Psychology*, volume 49, 2008.

[317] Dobre, O., "Employee motivation and organizational performance", *Review of Applied Socio-Economic Research*, volume 5, 2013.

[318] Chandola, T., and Zhang, N., "Re-employment, job quality, health and allostatic load bio-markers: Prospective evidence from the UK Household Longitudinal Study", *International Journal of Epidemiology*, August 2017.

[319] West, D. J., *Employee Engagement*, 2012.

[320] Izuma, K. and Saito D. N., "Processing of Social and Monetary Rewards in the Human Striatum", *Neuron*, volume 58, 2008.

[321] Martin Dewhurst, Matthew Guthridge, and Elizabeth Mohr, "Motivating People: Getting Beyond the Money", *McKinsey Quarterly*, November 2009.

[322] Murayama, K., et. el., "Neural basis of the undermining effect of monetary reward on intrinsic motivation", *Proceedings of the National Academy of Sciences*, volume 107, 2010.

[323] Lepper. M. R., Greene, D., and Nisbett, R. E., "Undermining children's intrinsic interest with extrinsic reward: A test of the 'over-justification' hypothesis", *Journal of Personality and Social Psychology*, volume 28, 1973.

[324] Judge, T., A., et. al., "The relationship between job pay and job satisfaction: A meta-analysis of the literature", *Journal of Vocational Behavior*, volume 77, 2010.

[325] McClelland, D.C., Atkinson, J.W., Clark, R.A., and Lowell, E.L., *The Achievement Motive*. Appleton-Century-Crofts, 1953.

[326] McClelland, D. C., *The Achieving Society*, Van Nostrand, 1961.

[327] Sutton, R., *The Asshole Survival Guide: How to deal with people who treat you like dirt,* Penguin Random House, 2017.

[328] Bock, L., *Work Rules: Insights from inside Google that will transform how you live and lead*, Twelve, 2015.

[329] Hackman, R., *Leading teams, setting the stage for great performances*, Harvard Business School Press, 2002.

[330] Hackman, R., *Groups that work (and those that don't)*, Jossey-Bass,1990.

[331] Cross, R., "Managing collaboration in the workplace effectively", *Babson College Executive Education,* January 2018.

[332] Woolley, A. W., et. al., "Evidence for a collective intelligence factor in the performance of human groups", *Science*, October 2010

[333] Cooke, N. J., et. al., "Interactive team cognition", *Cognitive Science*, volume 37, 2013.

[334] Barsade, S. G., "The Ripple Effect: Emotional Contagion and its Influence on Group Behaviour", *Administrative Science Quarterly*, volume 47, 2002.

[335] Felps, W., Mitchell, T., and Byington, E., "How, when, and why bad apples spoilt the barrel: Negative group members and dysfunctional groups, *Research in Organizational Behavior*, volume 27, 2006.

[336] Partington, D., and Harris, H., "Team role balance and team performance: An empirical study", *Journal of Management Development*, volume 18, 1999.

[337] Mesmer-Magnus, J. R., and DeChurch, L. A., "Information sharing and team performance: A meta-analysis", *Journal of Applied Psychology*, volume 94, 2009.

[338] Wooley, A. W., et. al., "Evidence for a collective intelligence factor in the performance of human groups", *Science*, volume 330, 2010.

[339] Zautra, E. K., et. al., "Can we learn to treat one another better? A test of a social intelligence curriculum", *PMC* published on line June 15, 2015.

[340] Zipkin, A., "The wisdom of thoughtfulness", *New York Times*, May 31, 2000.

[341] Mesmer-Magnus, 2009, op.cit.

[342] Wooley, A., and Malone, T. W., "What makes a team smarter? More women", *Harvard Business Review*, June 2011/

[343] Williams, M., and Polman, E., "Is it me or her? How gender composition evokes interpersonally sensitive behavior on collaborative cross-boundary projects", *Organization Science*, volume 26, 2014.

[344] Edmondson, A., "Psychological safety and learning behavior in work teams", *Administrative Science Quarterly*, volume 44, 1999.

[345] Duhigg, C., "What Google learned from its quest to build the perfect team", *New York Times*, February 25, 2016.

[346] Hildreth, J. A. D., and Anderson, C., "Failure at the top: How power undermines collaborative performance", *Journal of personality and Social Psychology*, 2016.

[347] Katzenbach, J. R., and Smith, D. K., *The Wisdom of Teams*, Harvard Business School Press, 1993.

[348] Vogel, A. L., et.al., "Pioneering the transdisciplinary team science approach: Lessons learned from National Cancer Institute grantees", *Journal of Translational Medicine & Epidemiology*, volume 2, 2014.

[349] Qiu, T., et. al., "Performance of Cross-Functional Development Teams; A Multi-Level Mediated Model", *Journal of Product Innovation Management*, volume 26, 2009.

[350] deWit, F. R., Greer, L. L., and K.A. Jehn, K. A., "The paradox of intergroup conflict: A metaanalysis", *Journal of Applied Psychology*, volume 97, 2012.

[351] M. A. Marks, M.A., Mathieu, J.E., and Zaccaro, S. J., "A temporally based framework and taxonomy of team processes", *Academy of Management Review*, volume 26, 2001.

[352] Edmondson, A. C., "Psychological safety and learning behavior in work teams", *Administrative Science Quarterly*, volume 44, 1999.

[353] Pritchard, R. D., et. al., "The productivity measurement and enhancement system: A meta-analysis", *Journal of Applied Psychology*, volume 93, 2008.

[354] Losada, M., and Heaphy, E., "The Role of Positivity and Connectivity in the Performance of Business Teams: A Nonlinear Dynamics Model", *American Behavioural Scientist*, volume 47, 2004.

[355] Harris, A., "Distributed Leadership: According to the Evidence", *Journal of Educational Administration*, volume 46, 2008.

[356] Katzenbach and Smith, 1993.

44782718R00114

Printed in Poland
by Amazon Fulfillment
Poland Sp. z o.o., Wrocław